A WHO HQ GRAPHIC NOVEL

Who Was the Greatest?

MUHAMMAD ALI

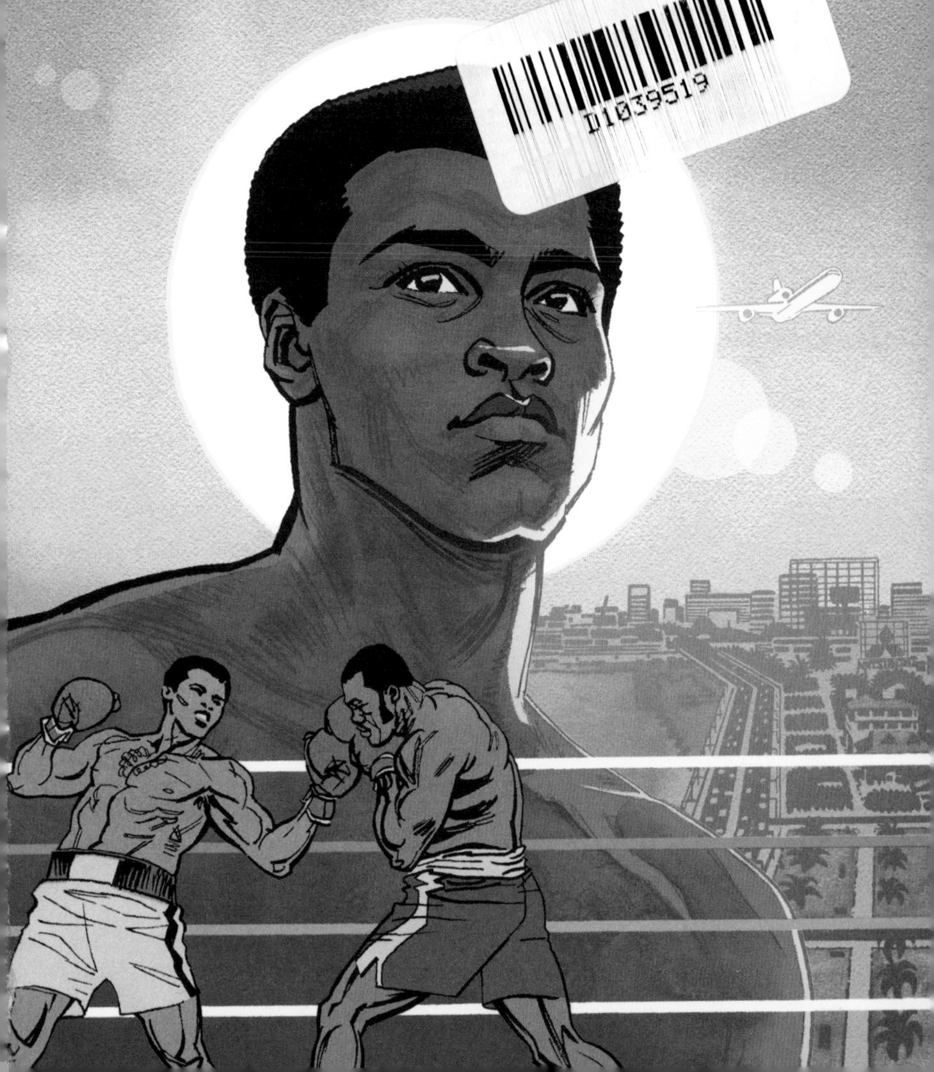

For Damon Bingham—GS

For Mom & Pop—CB

For Janis—RR

PENGUIN WORKSHOP
An Imprint of Penguin Random House LLC, New York

Penguin supports copyright. Copyright fuels creativity, encourages diverse voices, promotes free speech, and creates a vibrant culture. Thank you for buying an authorized edition of this book and for complying with copyright laws by not reproducing, scanning, or distributing any part of it in any form without permission. You are supporting writers and allowing Penguin to continue to publish books for every reader.

The publisher does not have any control over and does not assume any responsibility for author or third-party websites or their content.

Copyright © 2022 by Penguin Random House LLC. All rights reserved.
Published by Penguin Workshop, an imprint of Penguin Random House LLC, New York.
PENGUIN and PENGUIN WORKSHOP are trademarks of Penguin Books Ltd.
WHO HQ & Design is a registered trademark of Penguin Random House LLC.
Printed in the United States of America.

Visit us online at www.penguinrandomhouse.com.

Library of Congress Cataloging-in-Publication Data is available upon request.

ISBN 9780593224625 (pbk)   10 9 8 7 6 5 4 3 2 1 WOR
ISBN 9780593224632 (hc)   10 9 8 7 6 5 4 3 2 1 WOR

Lettering by Comicraft
Design by Mary Claire Cruz

This is a work of nonfiction. All of the events that unfold in the narrative are rooted in historical fact. Some dialogue and characters have been fictionalized in order to illustrate or teach a historical point.

For more information about your favorite historical figures, places, and events, please visit www.whohq.com.

A WHO HQ GRAPHIC NOVEL

Who Was the Greatest?

MUHAMMAD ALI

by Gabe Soria
illustrated by Chris Brunner
colors by Rico Renzi

Penguin Workshop

Introduction

Cassius Marcellus Clay Jr.—later known as Muhammad Ali—was born on January 17, 1942, in Louisville, Kentucky, to Cassius Clay Sr. and Odessa Grady Clay. In 1954, when he was twelve years old, he took up the sport of boxing after the theft of his bike by a bully, and by the time he was eighteen, he had won the gold medal in the light-heavyweight division at the 1960 Summer Olympics in Rome, Italy. After the Olympics, he became a professional boxer and quickly gained a notorious reputation, thanks to his outspoken attitude, brash confidence, and entertaining showmanship. In 1964, at the age of twenty-two, he defeated reigning American boxing legend Sonny Liston and became the boxing heavyweight champion of the world.

That same year, Cassius announced his conversion to the religion of Islam and changed his name to Muhammad Ali, and in 1967, he became a symbol of the anti-war movement when he refused being drafted into the United States Army to fight in the Vietnam War. As a result of his political stand, he was punished by boxing and government authorities alike, who took away his license to fight, stripped him of the heavyweight champion of the world title, and sentenced him to jail for draft evasion. He would not be able to fight professionally for the next few years, until 1970.

A year later, his conviction was overturned by the Supreme Court of the United States and his title was restored.

By 1975, Muhammad Ali was perhaps one of the most famous athletes in the world. His fighting career and his activism had made him a hero to some and an extremely controversial figure to others. So in September, when he found himself on a plane to Manila, the capital of the Philippines, to fight fellow heavyweight boxing superstar Joe Frazier, he wasn't entirely sure what to expect. This was the third in a series of fighting matches between Ali and Frazier that would determine who would be crowned the heavyweight champion. Ali lost the first match but triumphed in the second, so this third fight—the last fight, known as "the Thrilla in Manila"—meant everything. This was it.

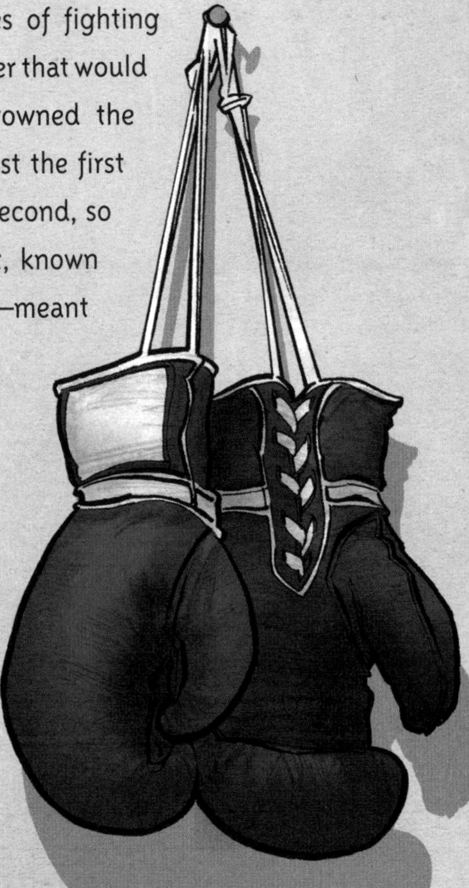

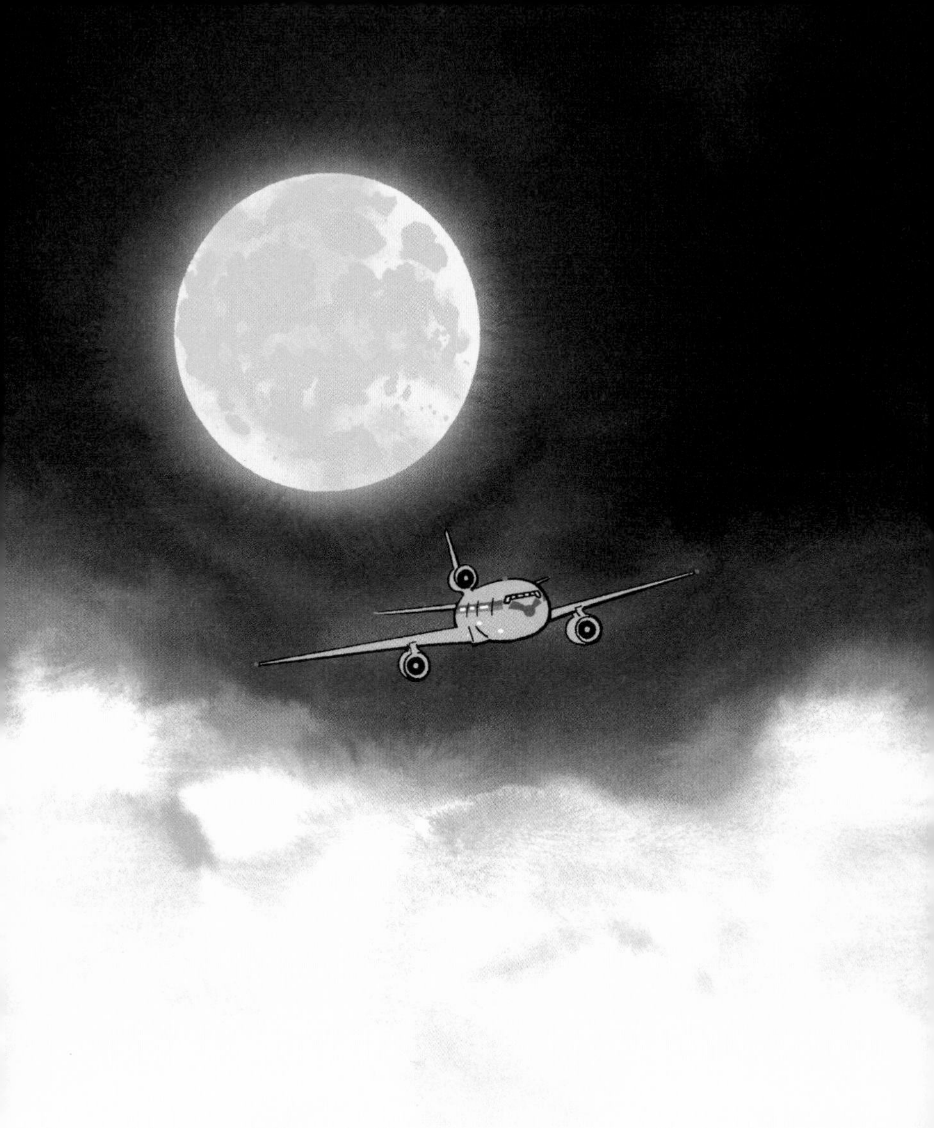

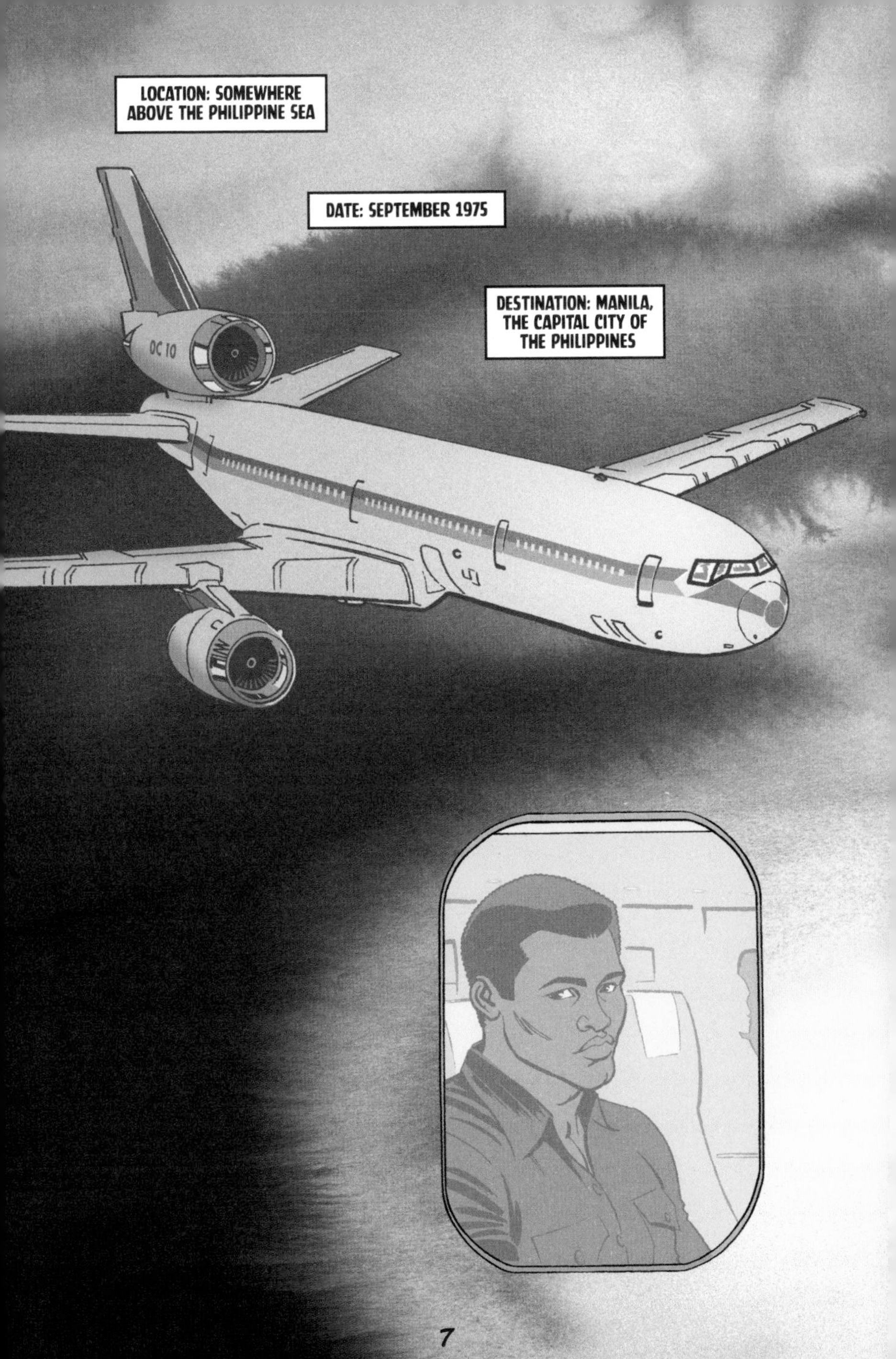
LOCATION: SOMEWHERE ABOVE THE PHILIPPINE SEA
DATE: SEPTEMBER 1975
DESTINATION: MANILA, THE CAPITAL CITY OF THE PHILIPPINES
DC 10

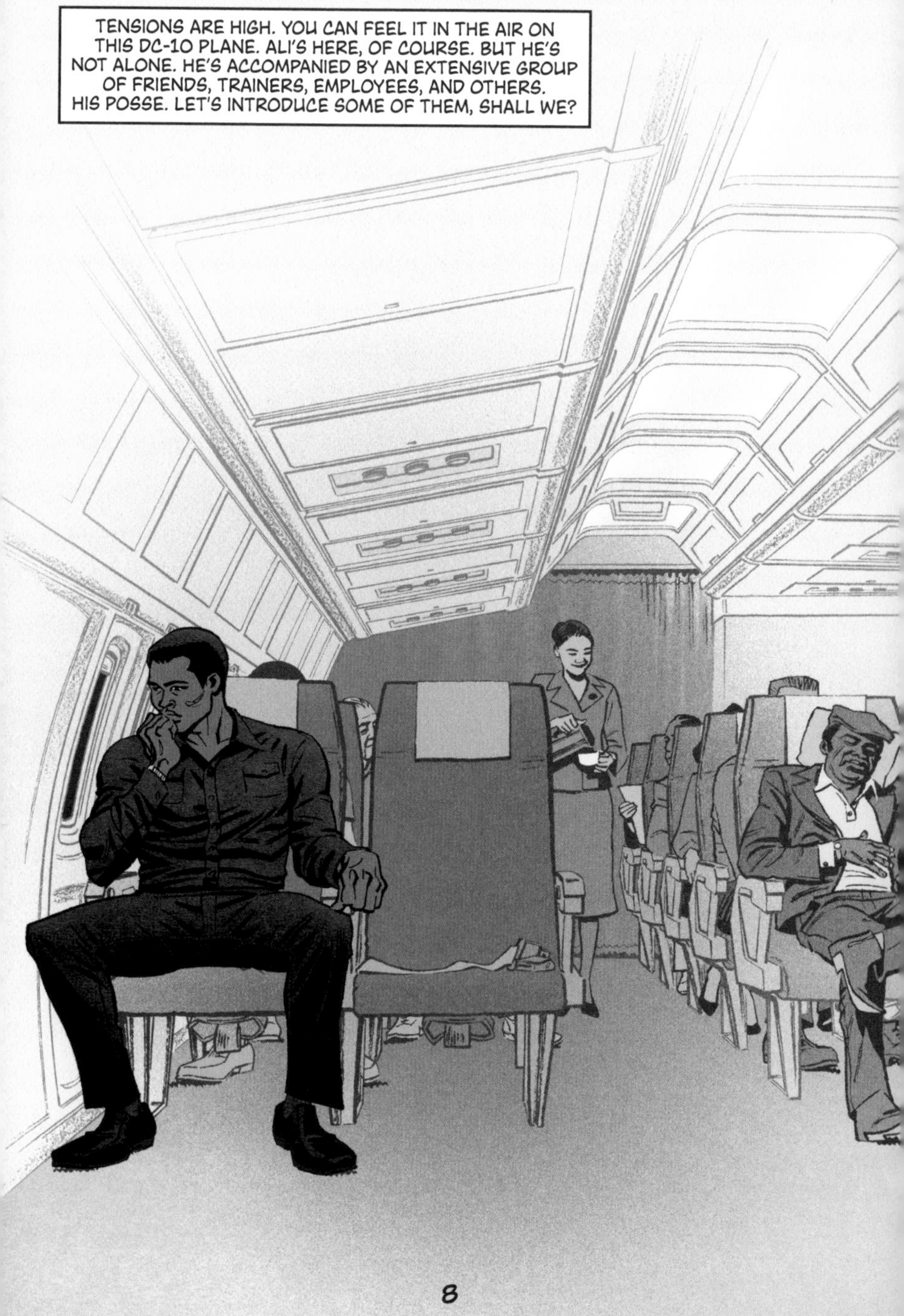
TENSIONS ARE HIGH. YOU CAN FEEL IT IN THE AIR ON THIS DC-10 PLANE. ALI'S HERE, OF COURSE. BUT HE'S NOT ALONE. HE'S ACCOMPANIED BY AN EXTENSIVE GROUP OF FRIENDS, TRAINERS, EMPLOYEES, AND OTHERS. HIS POSSE. LET'S INTRODUCE SOME OF THEM, SHALL WE?

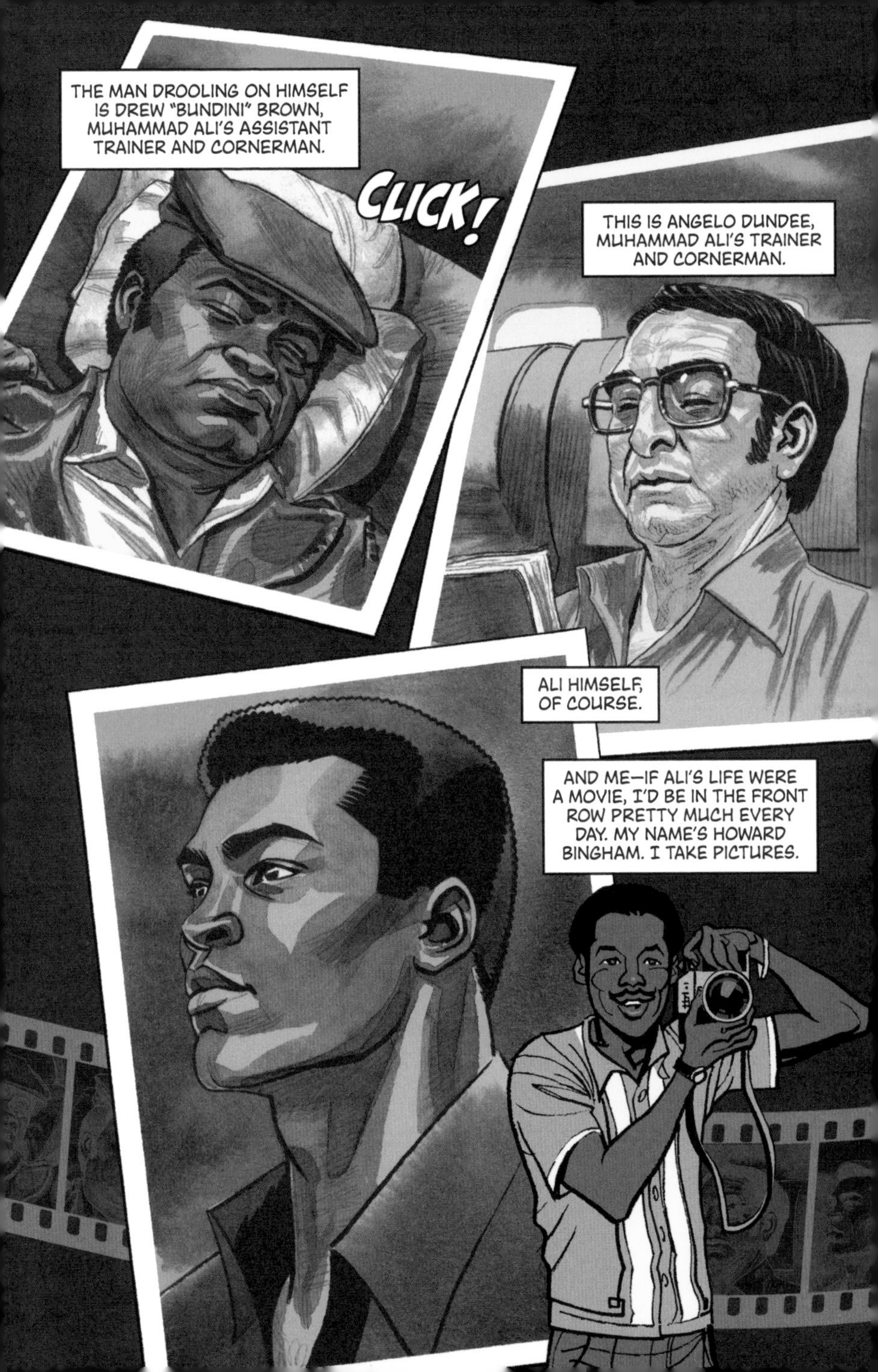
THE MAN DROOLING ON HIMSELF IS DREW "BUNDINI" BROWN, MUHAMMAD ALI'S ASSISTANT TRAINER AND CORNERMAN.
CLICK!
THIS IS ANGELO DUNDEE, MUHAMMAD ALI'S TRAINER AND CORNERMAN.
ALI HIMSELF, OF COURSE.
AND ME—IF ALI'S LIFE WERE A MOVIE, I'D BE IN THE FRONT ROW PRETTY MUCH EVERY DAY. MY NAME'S HOWARD BINGHAM. I TAKE PICTURES.

Howard Bingham

Born on May 29, 1939, in Jackson, Mississippi, Howard Bingham was Muhammad Ali's personal photographer as well as one of his closest confidantes. Bingham met Ali (as Cassius Clay) in 1962 in Los Angeles, while on assignment to cover the announcement of Clay's fight against George Logan. After the press conference, Bingham, originally from South Los Angeles, offered to serve as a tour guide to the city for Ali and his brother. That meeting was the beginning of a friendship that lasted more than fifty years. In addition to his work with Ali, Bingham photographed Malcolm X, the Black Panthers, and an almost endless list of actors and musicians, among other subjects.

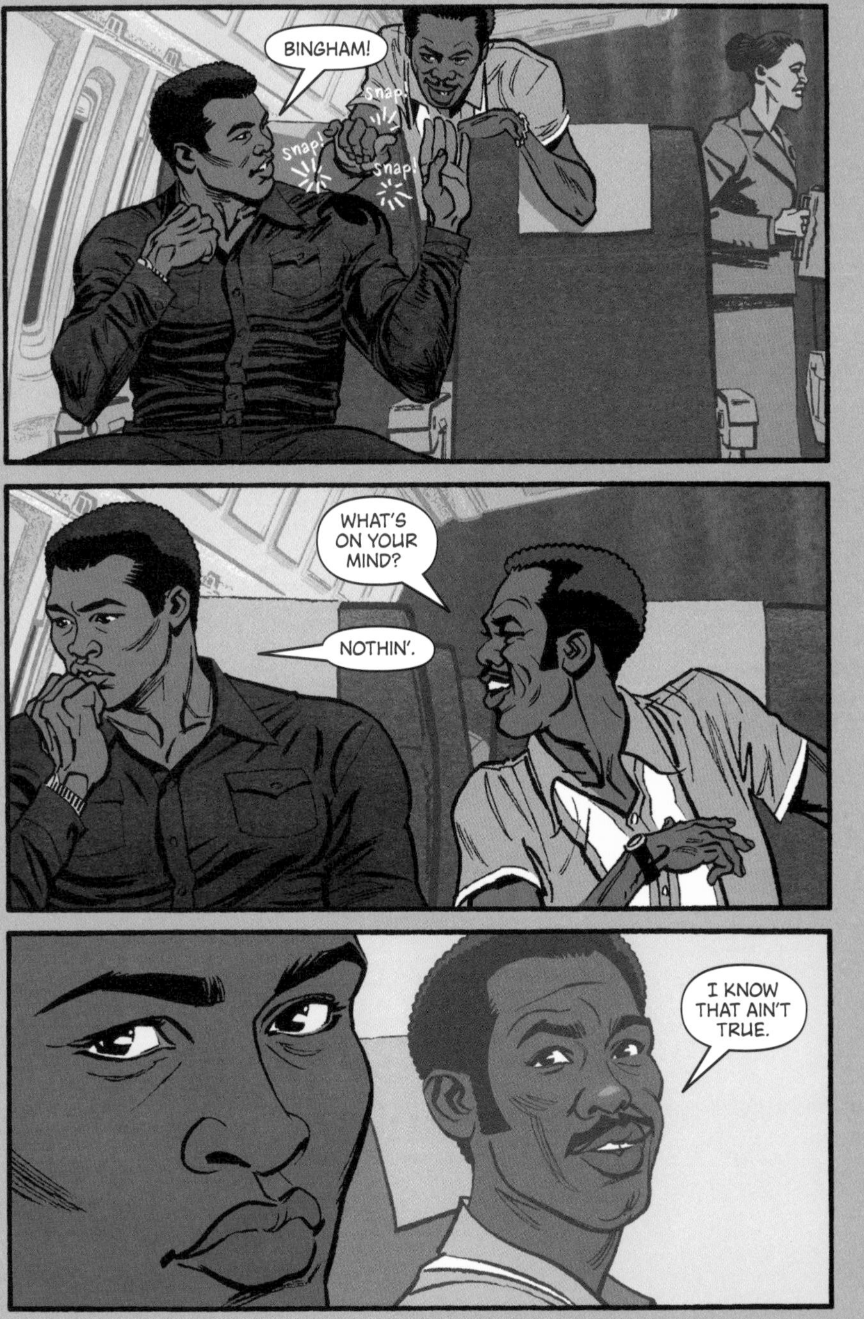
BINGHAM!
snap!
snap!
snap!
WHAT'S ON YOUR MIND?
NOTHIN'.
I KNOW THAT AIN'T TRUE.

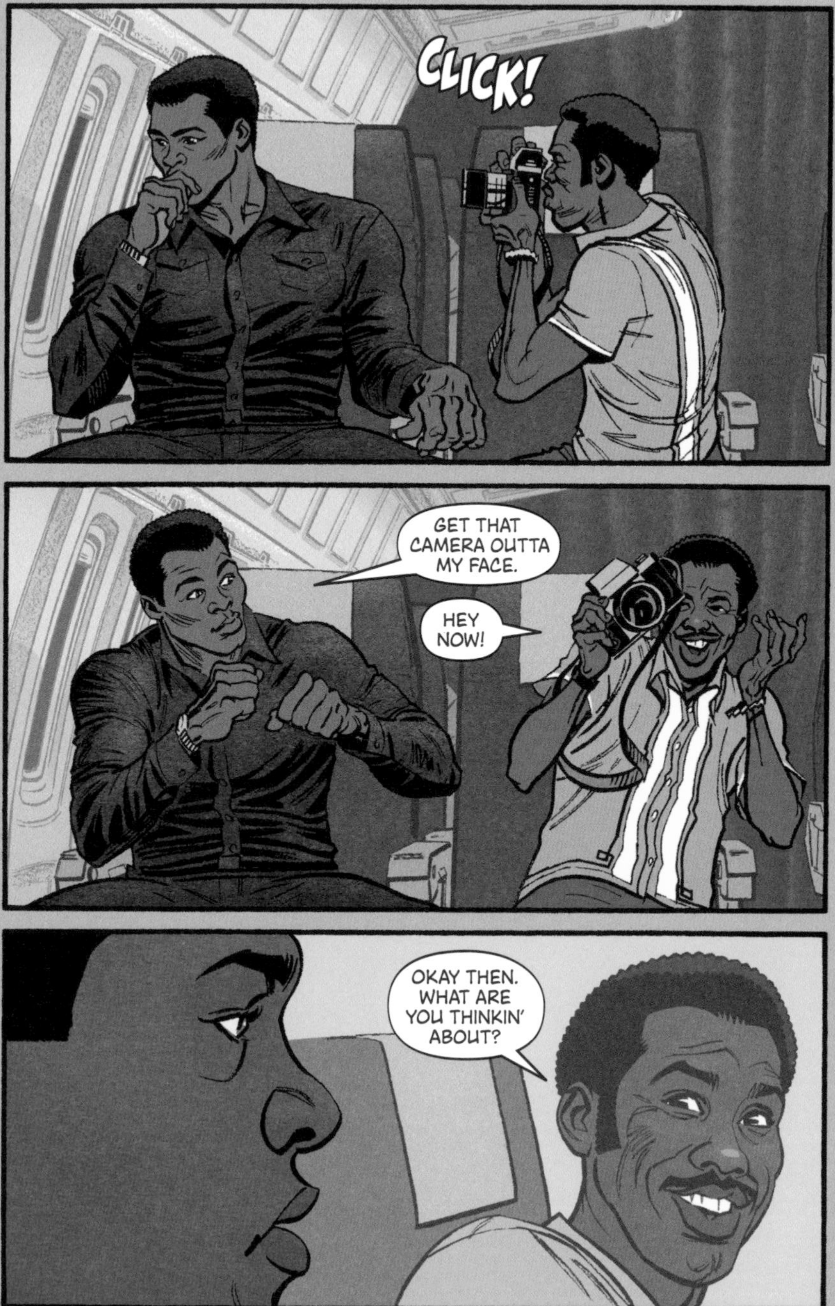
CLICK!
GET THAT CAMERA OUTTA MY FACE.
HEY NOW!
OKAY THEN. WHAT ARE YOU THINKIN' ABOUT?

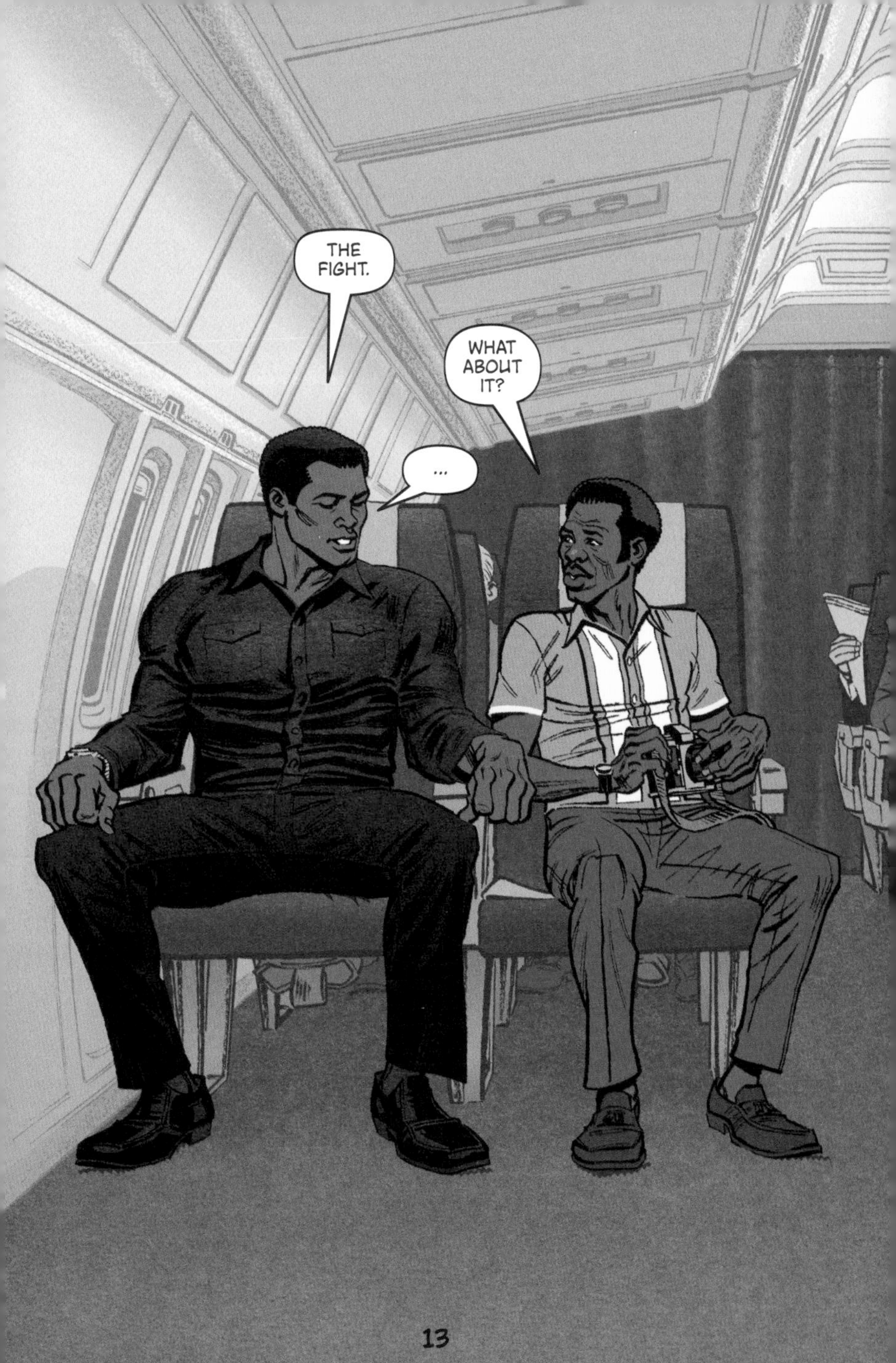
THE FIGHT.
WHAT ABOUT IT?
...

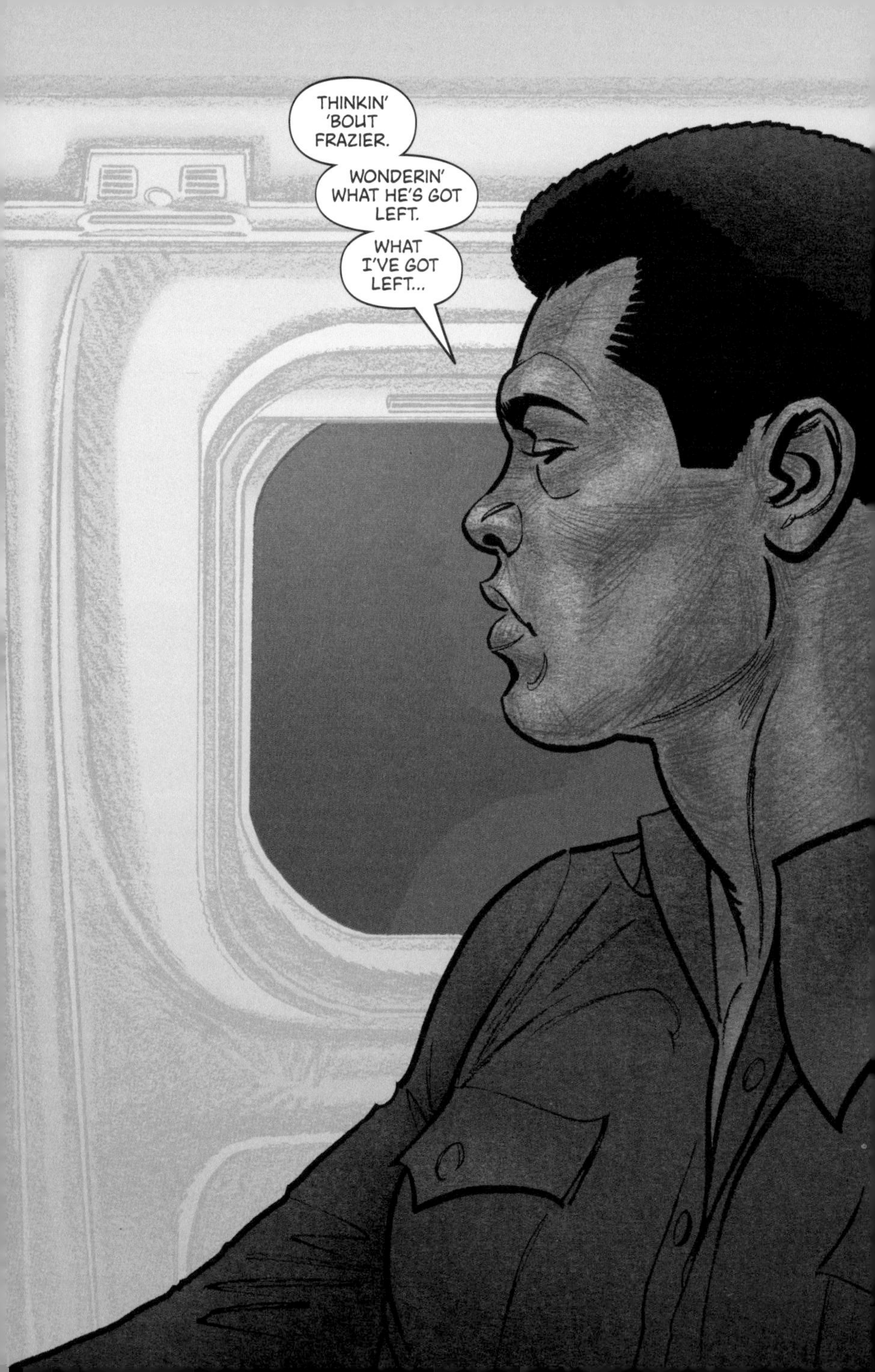
THINKIN' 'BOUT FRAZIER.
WONDERIN' WHAT HE'S GOT LEFT.
WHAT I'VE GOT LEFT...

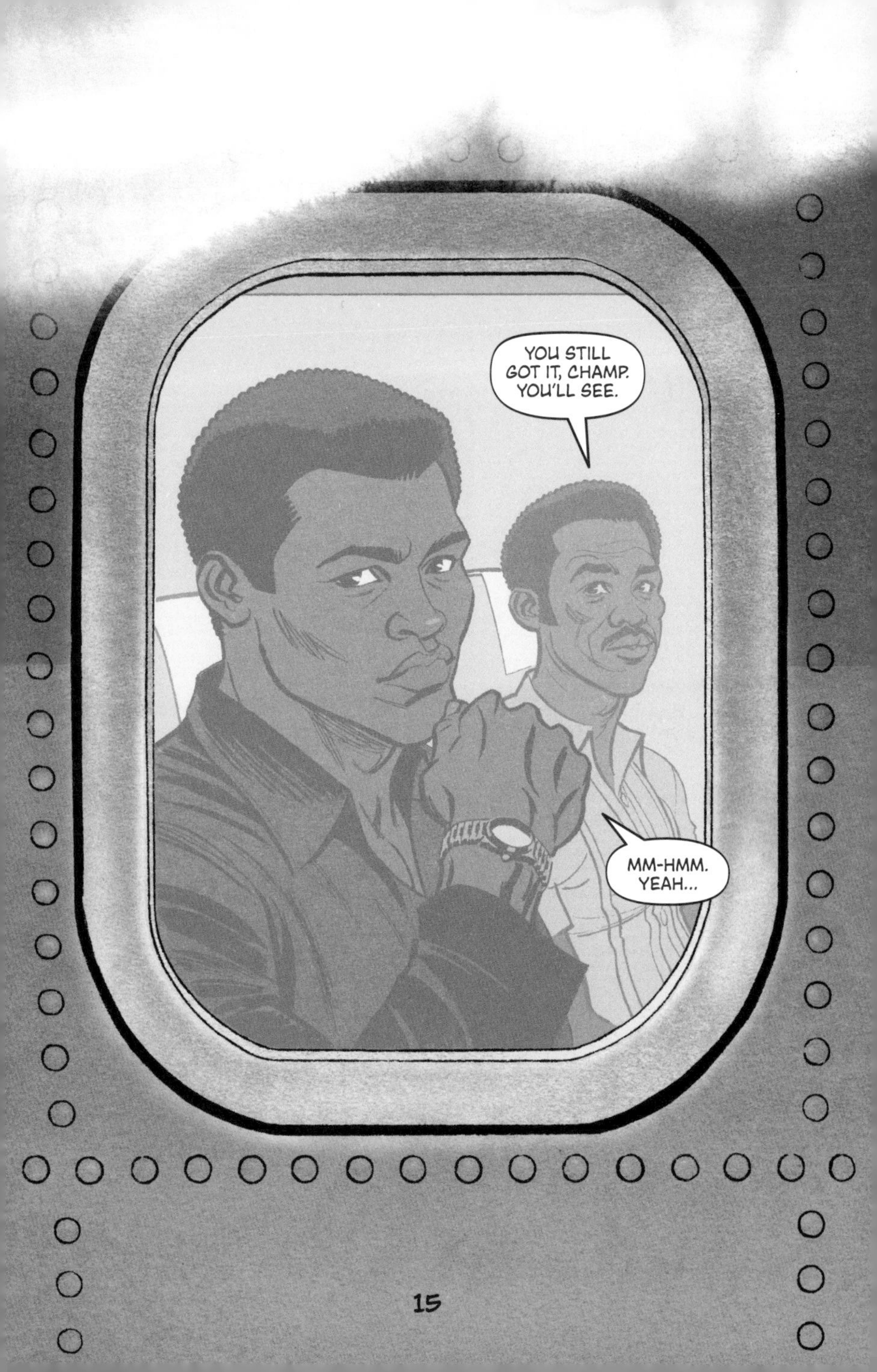
YOU STILL GOT IT, CHAMP. YOU'LL SEE.
MM-HMM. YEAH...

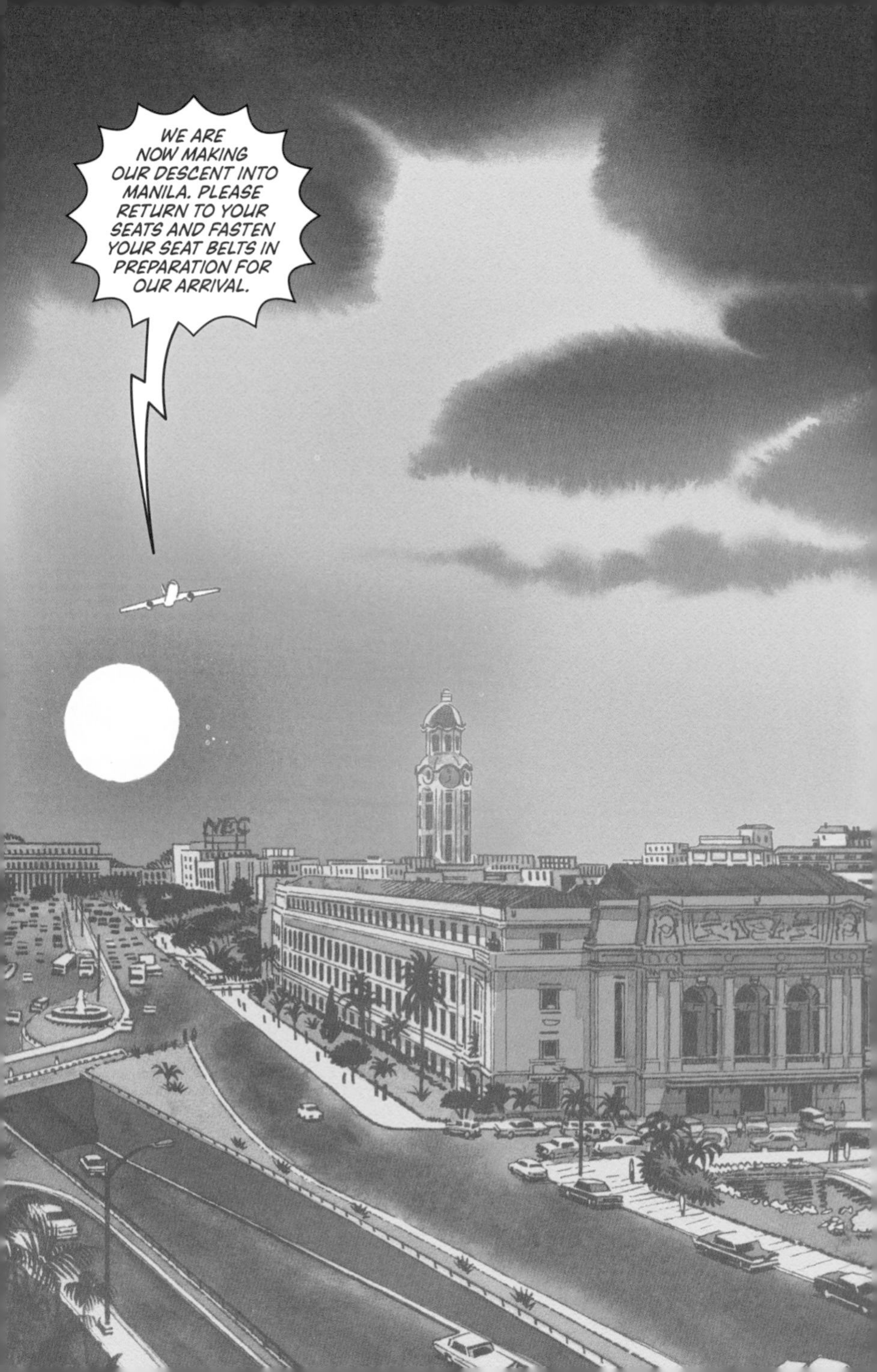
WE ARE NOW MAKING OUR DESCENT INTO MANILA. PLEASE RETURN TO YOUR SEATS AND FASTEN YOUR SEAT BELTS IN PREPARATION FOR OUR ARRIVAL.
NEC

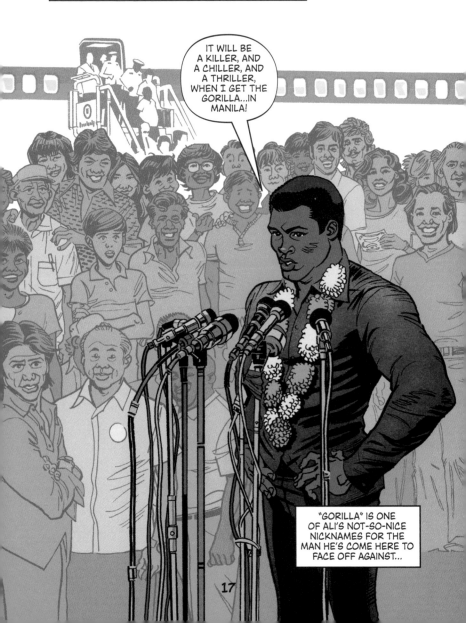

IT'S SEPTEMBER 15, 1975, WHEN WE LAND IN MANILA. THE FIGHT ISN'T HAPPENING FOR TWO WEEKS, BUT ALL THAT TIME WILL BE FILLED WITH TRAINING, PRESS CONFERENCES, AND PUBLIC APPEARANCES... THE FIGHT IS GOING TO BE A HUGE INTERNATIONAL EVENT, AND THE HYPE IS STARTING EARLY.

IT WILL BE A KILLER, AND A CHILLER, AND A THRILLER, WHEN I GET THE GORILLA...IN MANILA!

"GORILLA" IS ONE OF ALI'S NOT-SO-NICE NICKNAMES FOR THE MAN HE'S COME HERE TO FACE OFF AGAINST...

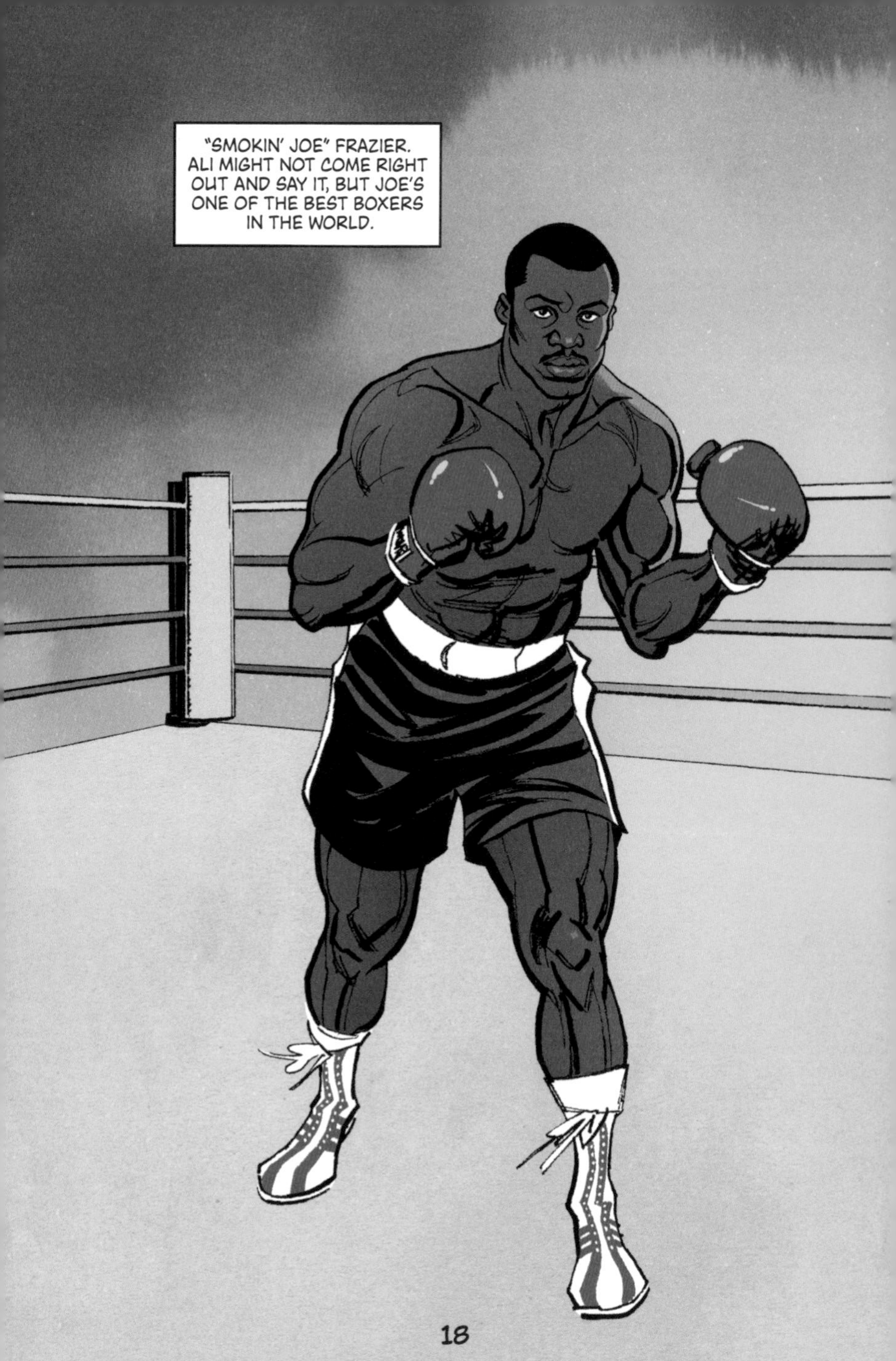
"SMOKIN' JOE" FRAZIER. ALI MIGHT NOT COME RIGHT OUT AND SAY IT, BUT JOE'S ONE OF THE BEST BOXERS IN THE WORLD.

Joe Frazier

Joe Frazier was born in Beaufort County, South Carolina, on January 12, 1944, where he was a member of the Gullah community. Feeling constricted by the racism he experienced while growing up, he moved north by himself when he was fifteen years old, first to New York City and then to Philadelphia, where he began to train as a boxer. Like Ali, he was a former Olympic boxer—he won a gold medal at the 1964 Summer Olympics in Tokyo—and also like Ali, he was the heavyweight boxing champion of the world, a title he held from 1970 to 1973. He was known by the nickname "Smokin' Joe," and he had been friends with Ali, but their relationship soured after Ali continued to insult him when they competed against each other. Frazier retired from professional boxing twice: once in 1976 and again after an unsuccessful comeback fight in 1981. Nine years later, he was inducted into the International Boxing Hall of Fame. In 2011, Frazier passed away from liver cancer at age sixty-seven. He is considered to be one of the greatest heavyweight boxers of all time.

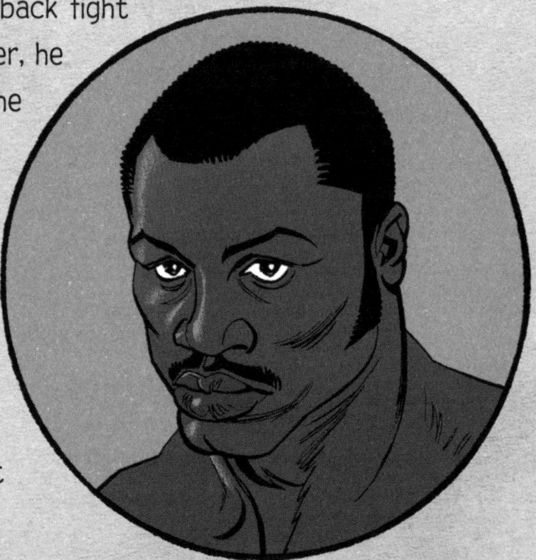

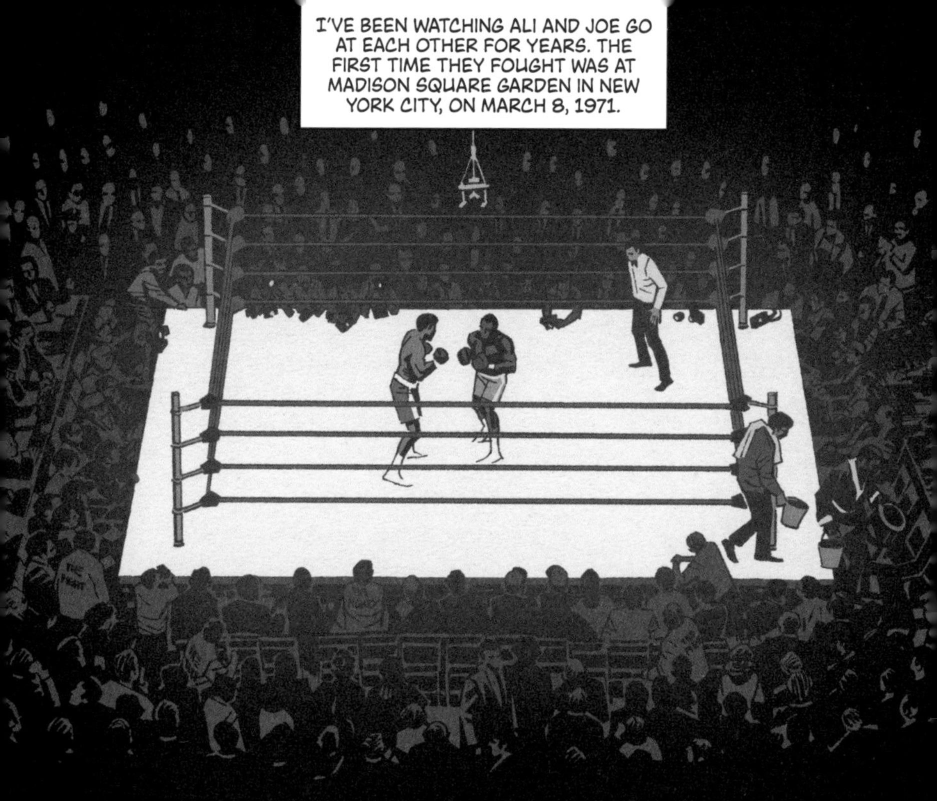
I'VE BEEN WATCHING ALI AND JOE GO AT EACH OTHER FOR YEARS. THE FIRST TIME THEY FOUGHT WAS AT MADISON SQUARE GARDEN IN NEW YORK CITY, ON MARCH 8, 1971.

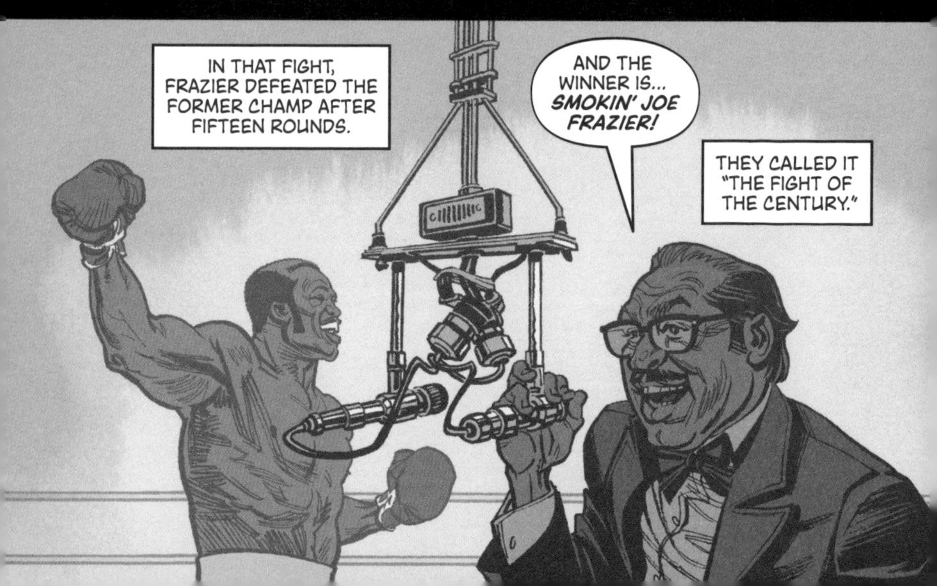
IN THAT FIGHT, FRAZIER DEFEATED THE FORMER CHAMP AFTER FIFTEEN ROUNDS.
AND THE WINNER IS... ***SMOKIN' JOE FRAZIER!***
THEY CALLED IT "THE FIGHT OF THE CENTURY."

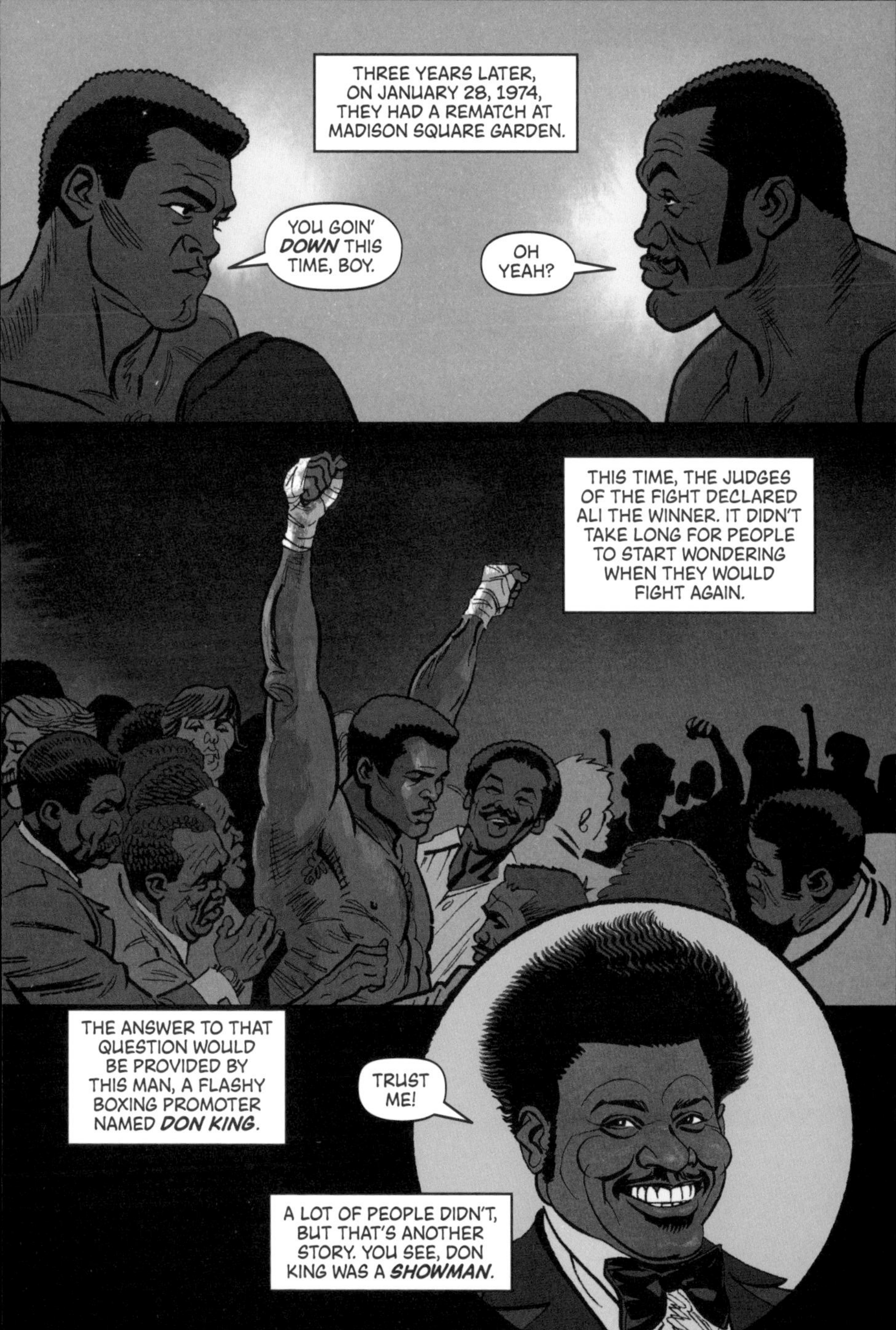
THREE YEARS LATER, ON JANUARY 28, 1974, THEY HAD A REMATCH AT MADISON SQUARE GARDEN.
YOU GOIN' **DOWN** THIS TIME, BOY.
OH YEAH?
THIS TIME, THE JUDGES OF THE FIGHT DECLARED ALI THE WINNER. IT DIDN'T TAKE LONG FOR PEOPLE TO START WONDERING WHEN THEY WOULD FIGHT AGAIN.
THE ANSWER TO THAT QUESTION WOULD BE PROVIDED BY THIS MAN, A FLASHY BOXING PROMOTER NAMED **DON KING**.
TRUST ME!
A LOT OF PEOPLE DIDN'T, BUT THAT'S ANOTHER STORY. YOU SEE, DON KING WAS A **SHOWMAN**.

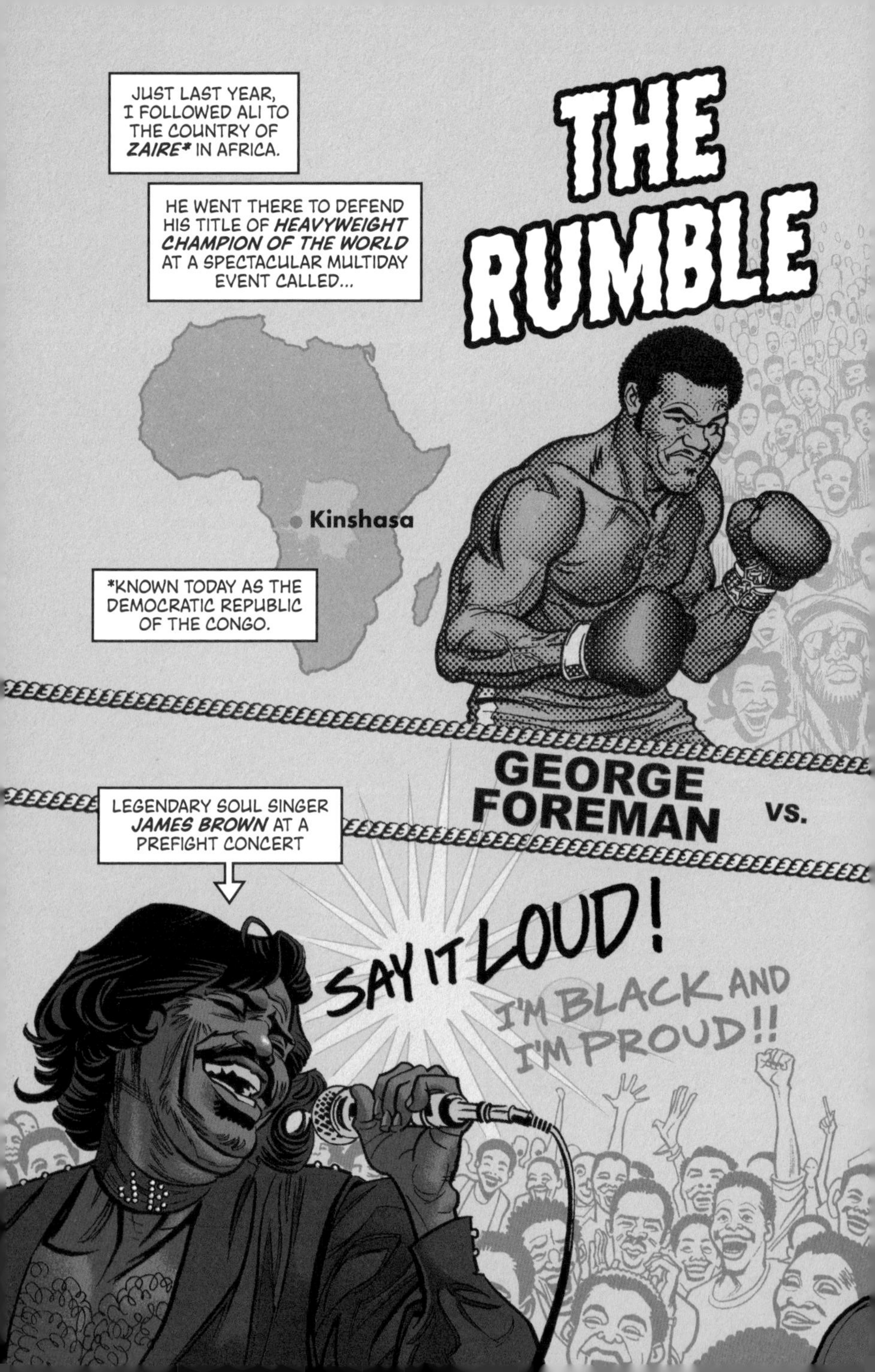

JUST LAST YEAR, I FOLLOWED ALI TO THE COUNTRY OF *ZAIRE** IN AFRICA.
HE WENT THERE TO DEFEND HIS TITLE OF ***HEAVYWEIGHT CHAMPION OF THE WORLD*** AT A SPECTACULAR MULTIDAY EVENT CALLED...
THE RUMBLE
Kinshasa
*KNOWN TODAY AS THE DEMOCRATIC REPUBLIC OF THE CONGO.
GEORGE FOREMAN
VS.
LEGENDARY SOUL SINGER *JAMES BROWN* AT A PREFIGHT CONCERT
SAY IT LOUD!
I'M BLACK AND I'M PROUD!!

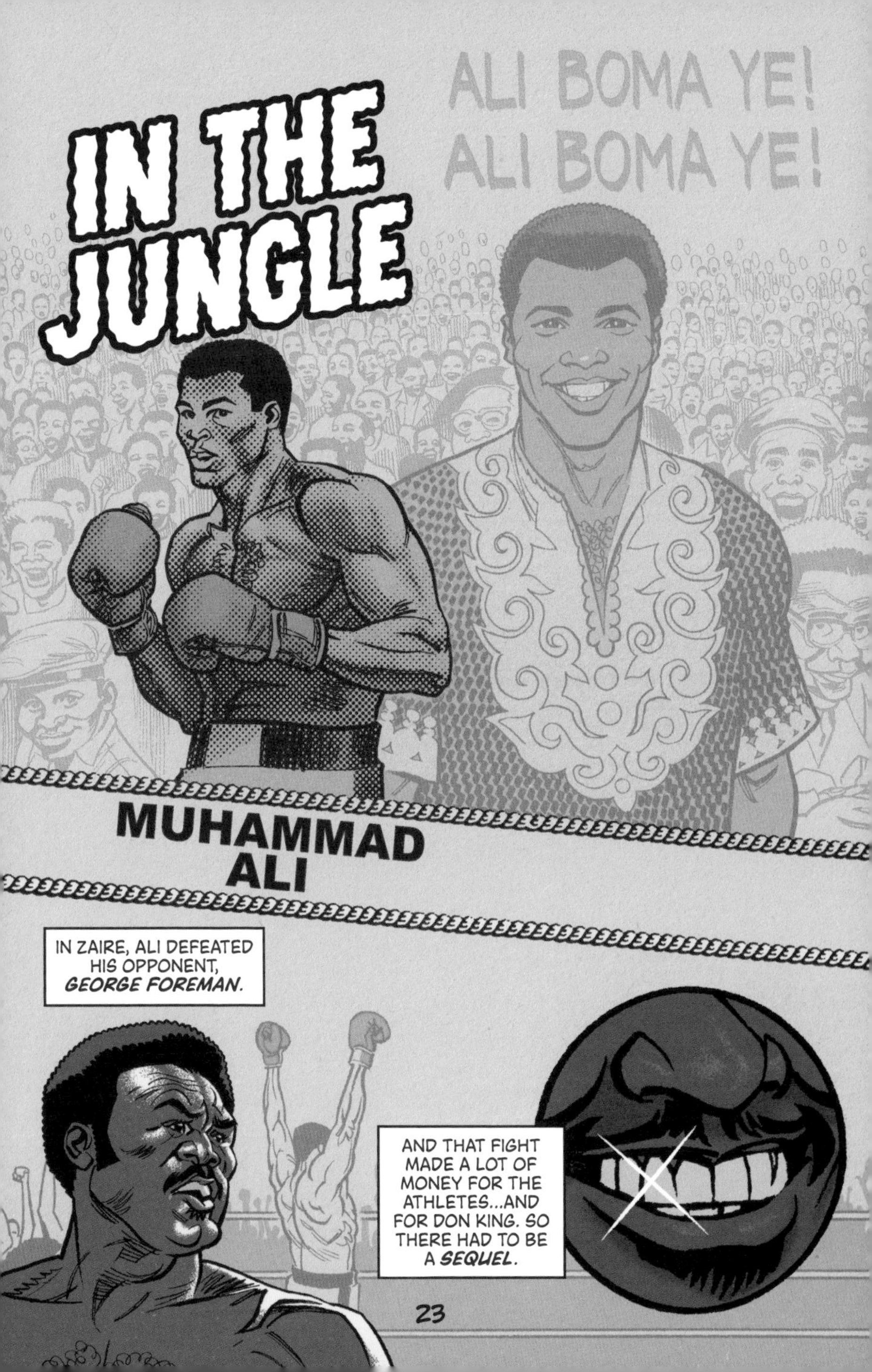
ALI BOMA YE!
ALI BOMA YE!
IN THE JUNGLE
MUHAMMAD ALI
IN ZAIRE, ALI DEFEATED HIS OPPONENT, *GEORGE FOREMAN*.
AND THAT FIGHT MADE A LOT OF MONEY FOR THE ATHLETES...AND FOR DON KING. SO THERE HAD TO BE A *SEQUEL*.

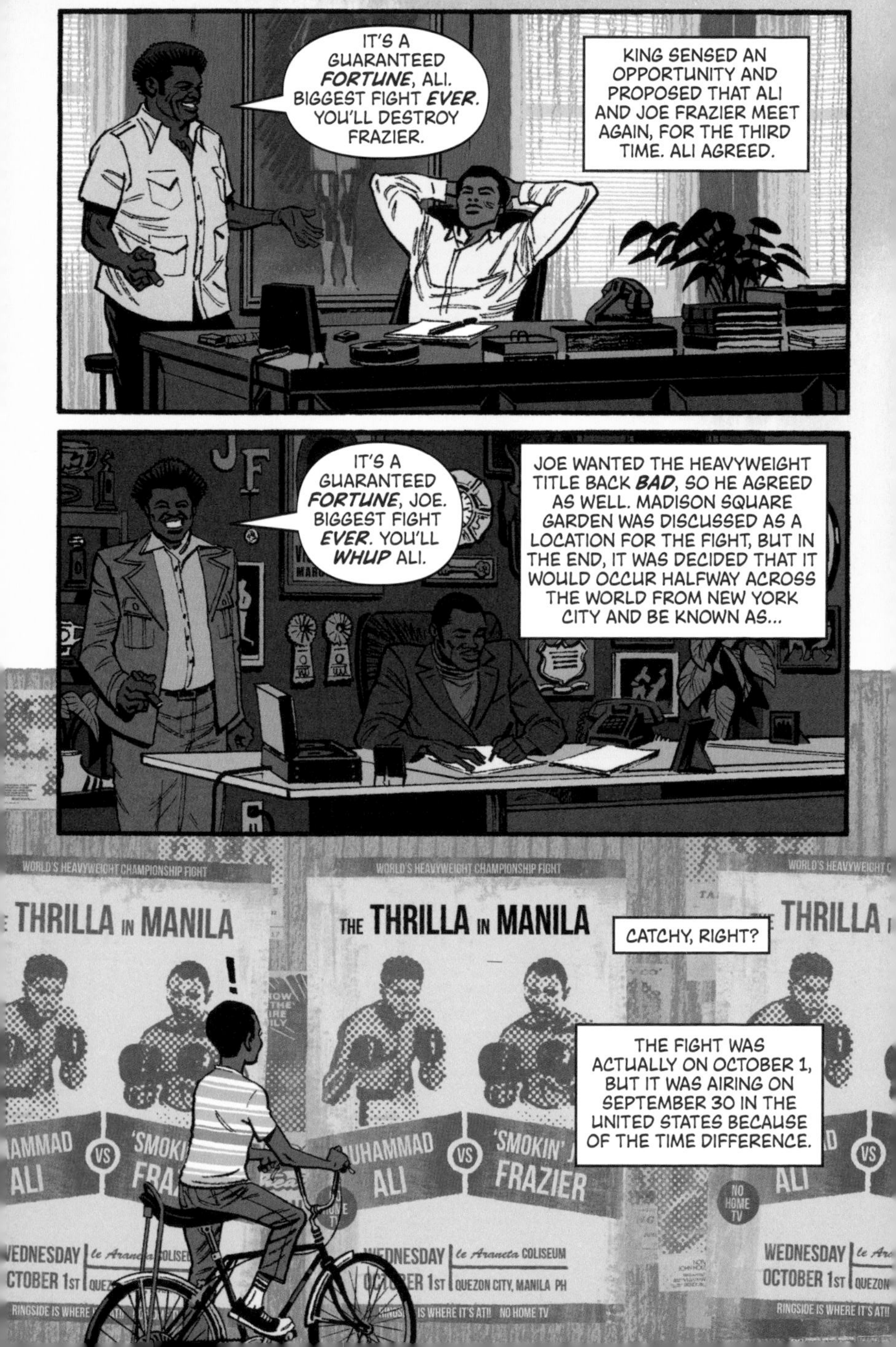
IT'S A GUARANTEED *FORTUNE*, ALI. BIGGEST FIGHT *EVER*. YOU'LL DESTROY FRAZIER.
KING SENSED AN OPPORTUNITY AND PROPOSED THAT ALI AND JOE FRAZIER MEET AGAIN, FOR THE THIRD TIME. ALI AGREED.
IT'S A GUARANTEED *FORTUNE*, JOE. BIGGEST FIGHT *EVER*. YOU'LL *WHUP* ALI.
JOE WANTED THE HEAVYWEIGHT TITLE BACK *BAD*, SO HE AGREED AS WELL. MADISON SQUARE GARDEN WAS DISCUSSED AS A LOCATION FOR THE FIGHT, BUT IN THE END, IT WAS DECIDED THAT IT WOULD OCCUR HALFWAY ACROSS THE WORLD FROM NEW YORK CITY AND BE KNOWN AS...
WORLD'S HEAVYWEIGHT CHAMPIONSHIP FIGHT
THE THRILLA IN MANILA
CATCHY, RIGHT?
!
THE FIGHT WAS ACTUALLY ON OCTOBER 1, BUT IT WAS AIRING ON SEPTEMBER 30 IN THE UNITED STATES BECAUSE OF THE TIME DIFFERENCE.
'SMOKIN'
FRAZIER
VS
NO HOME TV
WEDNESDAY
le Araneta COLISEUM
QUEZON CITY, MANILA PH
IS WHERE IT'S AT!! NO HOME TV
RINGSIDE IS WHERE IT'S AT!!

The Philippines

The group of islands called the Philippines were colonized by the Spanish Empire in 1565 and remained a Spanish colony until 1898. That same year, the Philippines became a colony of the United States after the conflict known as the Spanish-American War. In 1935, the Philippines became a commonwealth—meaning that, though it still remained under US control, it could elect its own government. In 1941, the country was invaded by the Empire of Japan, which occupied the Philippines until the end of World War II, four years later. The Philippines became an independent country in 1946, and during Muhammad Ali's visit to Manila, Ferdinand Marcos was the president of the Philippines. His regime was marked by widespread corruption and violent suppression of political dissent. In 1986, Marcos's twenty years of autocratic rule came to an end when Corazon Aquino was elected the eleventh president of the country, as well as its first female leader.

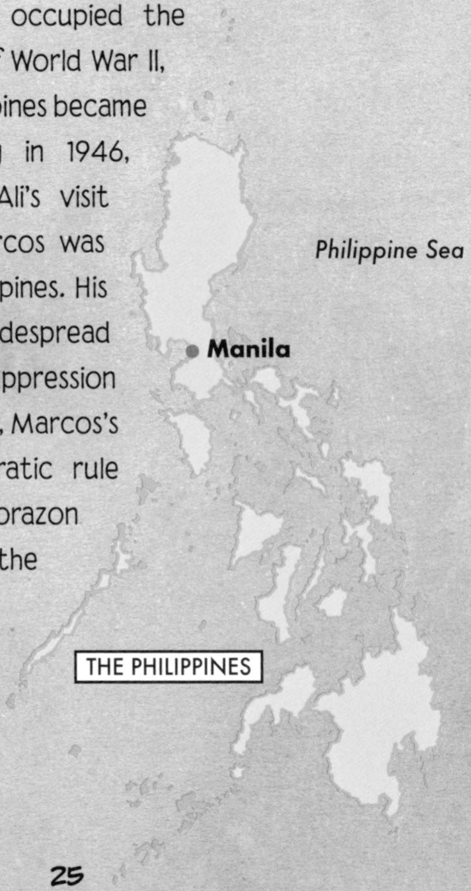
Philippine Sea
Manila
THE PHILIPPINES

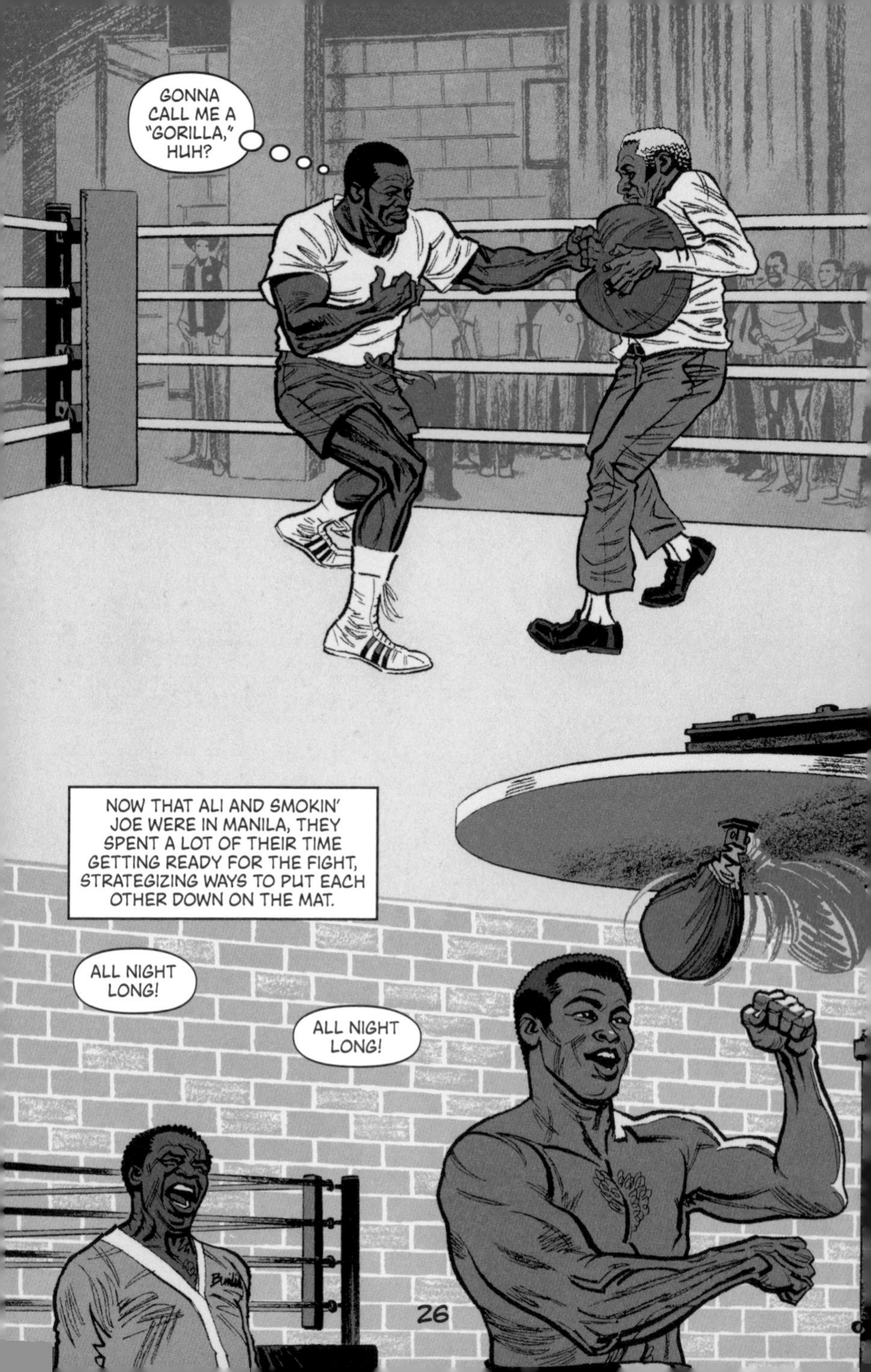
GONNA CALL ME A "GORILLA," HUH?
NOW THAT ALI AND SMOKIN' JOE WERE IN MANILA, THEY SPENT A LOT OF THEIR TIME GETTING READY FOR THE FIGHT, STRATEGIZING WAYS TO PUT EACH OTHER DOWN ON THE MAT.
ALL NIGHT LONG!
ALL NIGHT LONG!

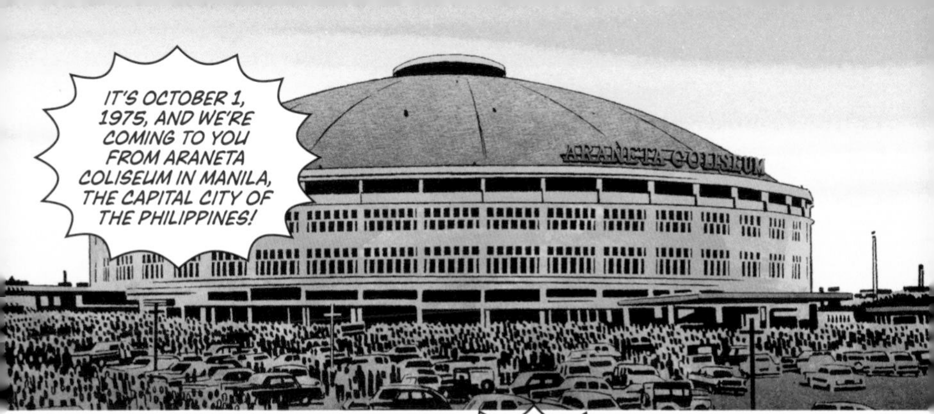
IT'S OCTOBER 1, 1975, AND WE'RE COMING TO YOU FROM ARANETA COLISEUM IN MANILA, THE CAPITAL CITY OF THE PHILIPPINES!
ARANETA COLISEUM

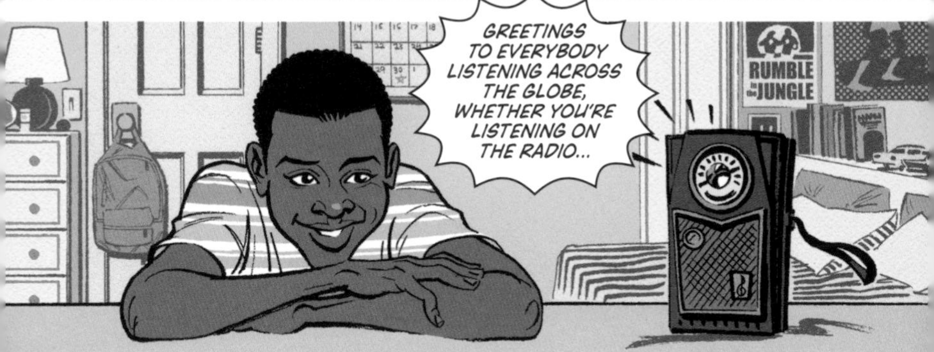
GREETINGS TO EVERYBODY LISTENING ACROSS THE GLOBE, WHETHER YOU'RE LISTENING ON THE RADIO...
RUMBLE in the JUNGLE

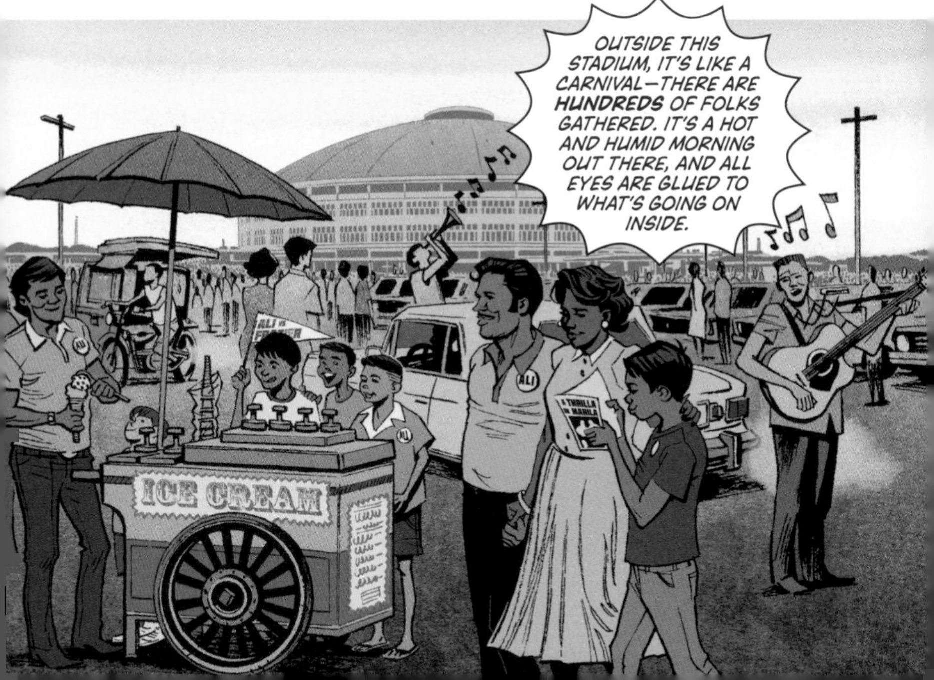
OUTSIDE THIS STADIUM, IT'S LIKE A CARNIVAL—THERE ARE **HUNDREDS** OF FOLKS GATHERED. IT'S A HOT AND HUMID MORNING OUT THERE, AND ALL EYES ARE GLUED TO WHAT'S GOING ON INSIDE.
ALI
A THRILLA in MANILA
ICE CREAM

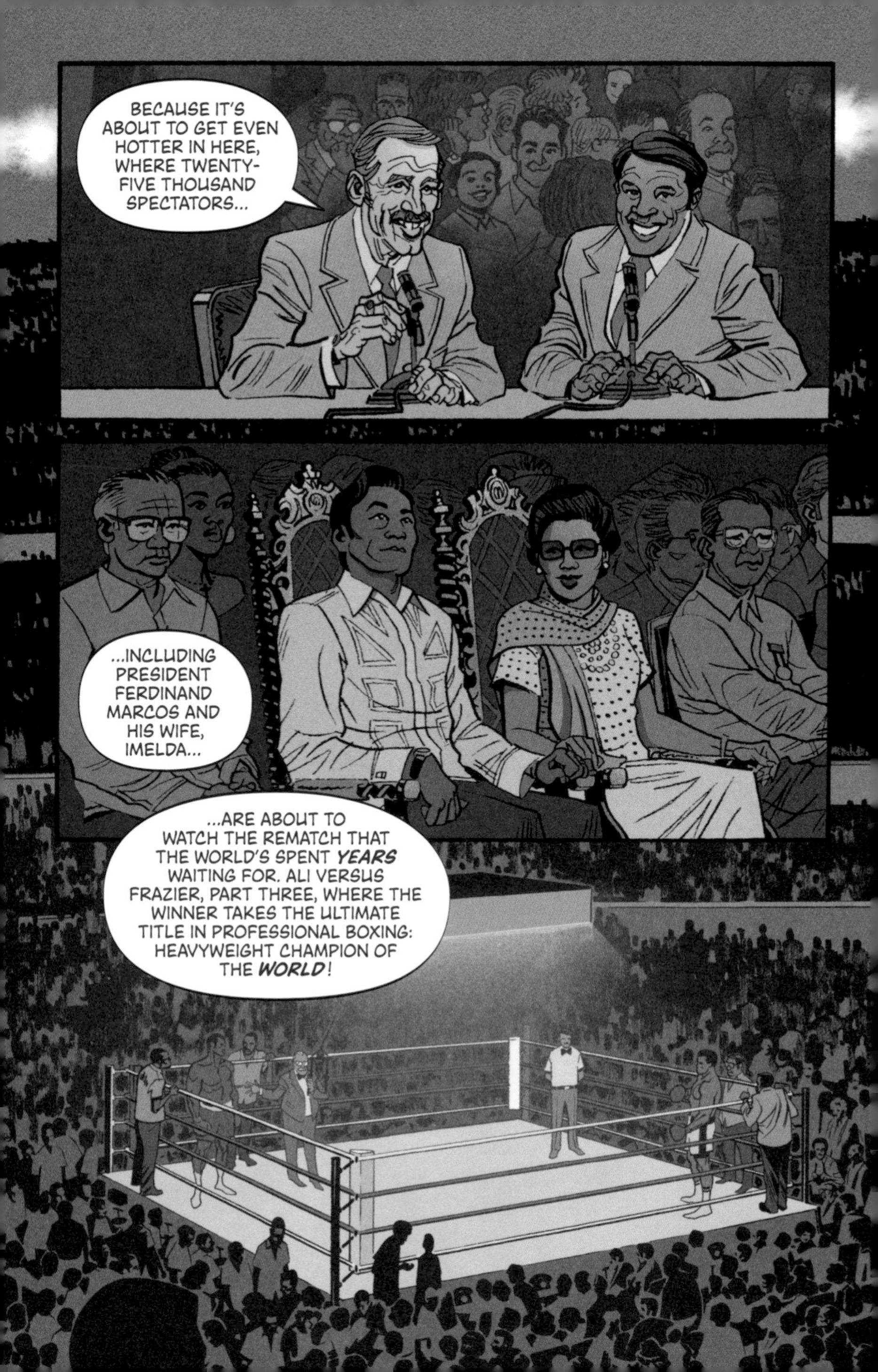

BECAUSE IT'S ABOUT TO GET EVEN HOTTER IN HERE, WHERE TWENTY-FIVE THOUSAND SPECTATORS...
...INCLUDING PRESIDENT FERDINAND MARCOS AND HIS WIFE, IMELDA...
...ARE ABOUT TO WATCH THE REMATCH THAT THE WORLD'S SPENT *YEARS* WAITING FOR. ALI VERSUS FRAZIER, PART THREE, WHERE THE WINNER TAKES THE ULTIMATE TITLE IN PROFESSIONAL BOXING: HEAVYWEIGHT CHAMPION OF THE *WORLD*!

Professional Boxing

Hand-to-hand combat and martial arts are a tradition in many cultures across the world, but the sport we know today as boxing most likely has its roots in ancient Egypt, Rome, and Greece—where it was an Olympic sport over two thousand years ago. Boxing was a violent activity that often resulted in fatalities. Modern boxing began to take shape in England in the seventeenth century, and it remains controversial due to its violent, though less fatal, nature. Today in boxing, both amateur and professional matches consist of up to twelve three-minute rounds and are usually held between people in the same weight range, also known as a weight class. As of 2020, there were seventeen weight classes in boxing, including strawweight (115 pounds or below), flyweight, (115 pounds to 125 pounds), lightweight (145 to 155 pounds), middleweight (175 to 185 pounds), and heavyweight (225 to 265 pounds).

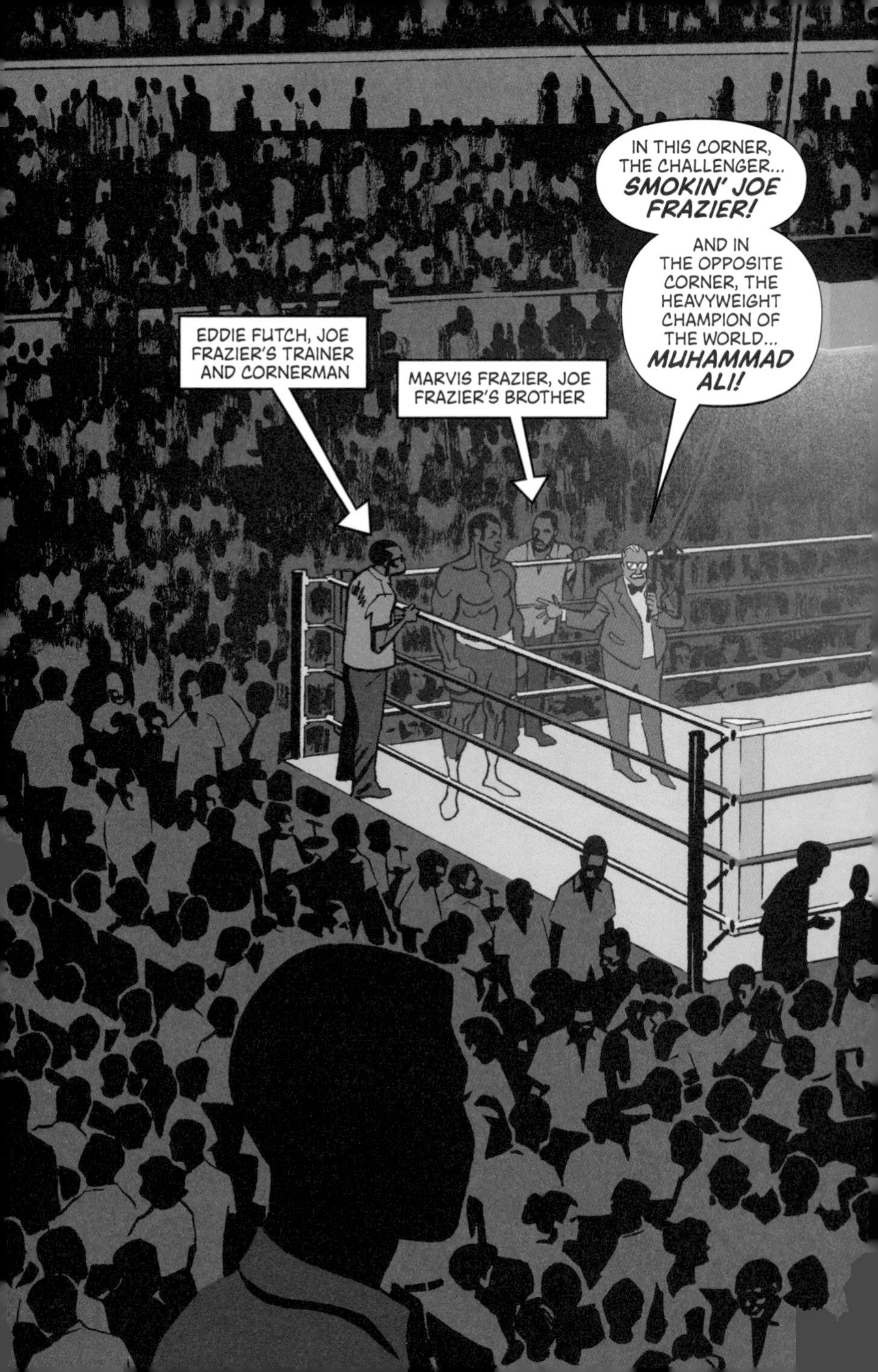
EDDIE FUTCH, JOE FRAZIER'S TRAINER AND CORNERMAN
MARVIS FRAZIER, JOE FRAZIER'S BROTHER
IN THIS CORNER, THE CHALLENGER... SMOKIN' JOE FRAZIER!
AND IN THE OPPOSITE CORNER, THE HEAVYWEIGHT CHAMPION OF THE WORLD... MUHAMMAD ALI!

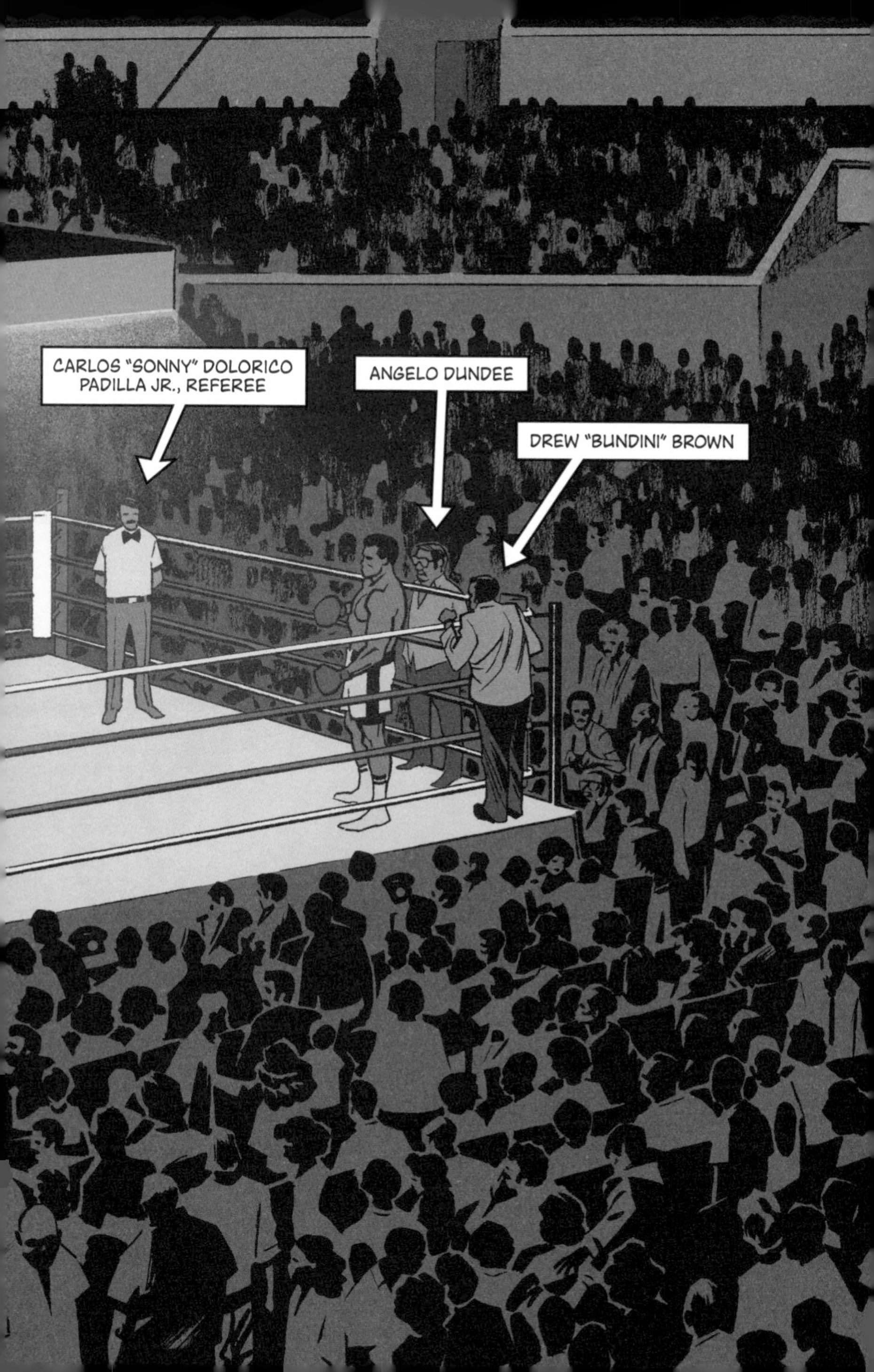
CARLOS "SONNY" DOLORICO PADILLA JR., REFEREE
ANGELO DUNDEE
DREW "BUNDINI" BROWN

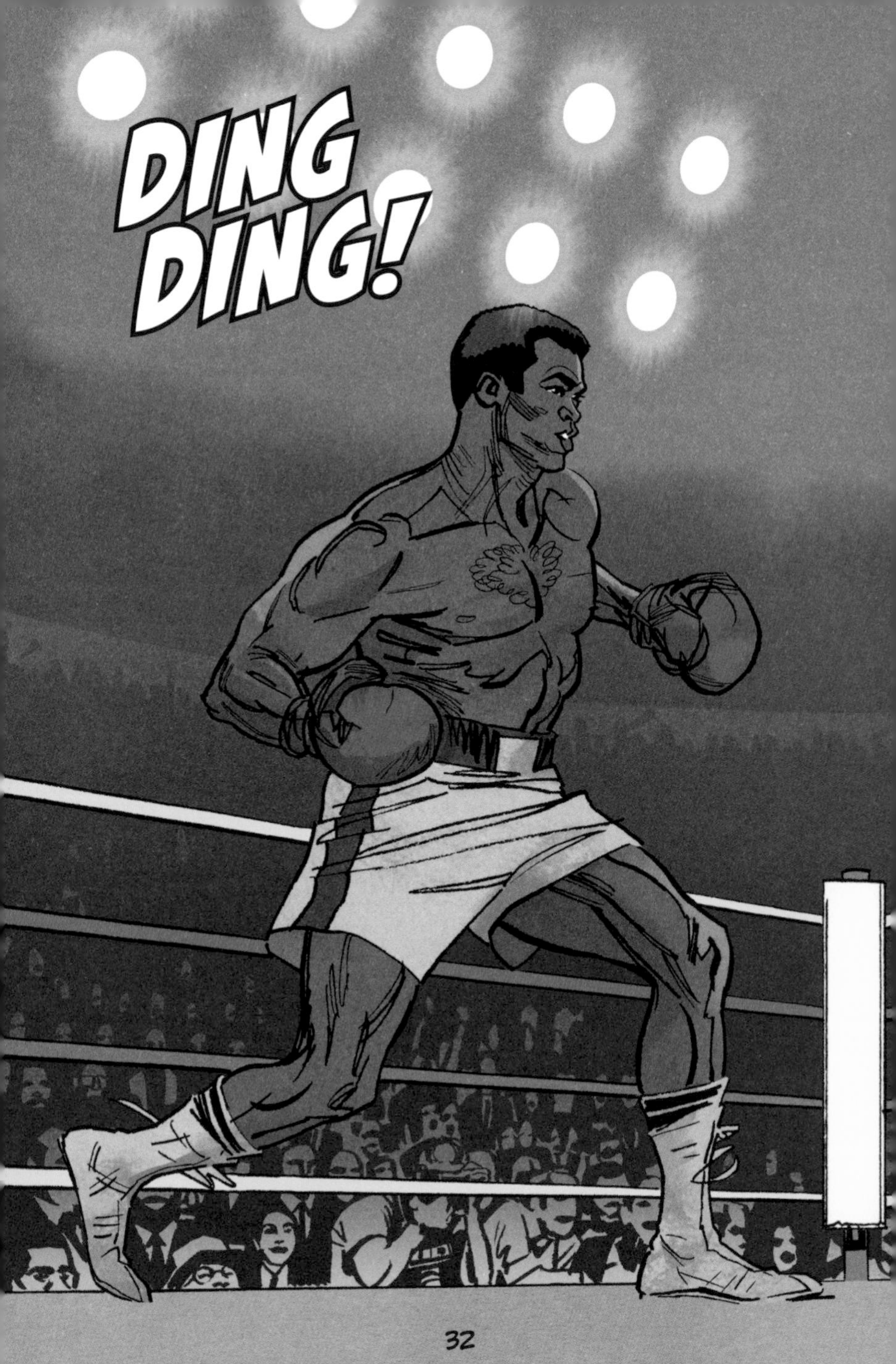
DING DING!

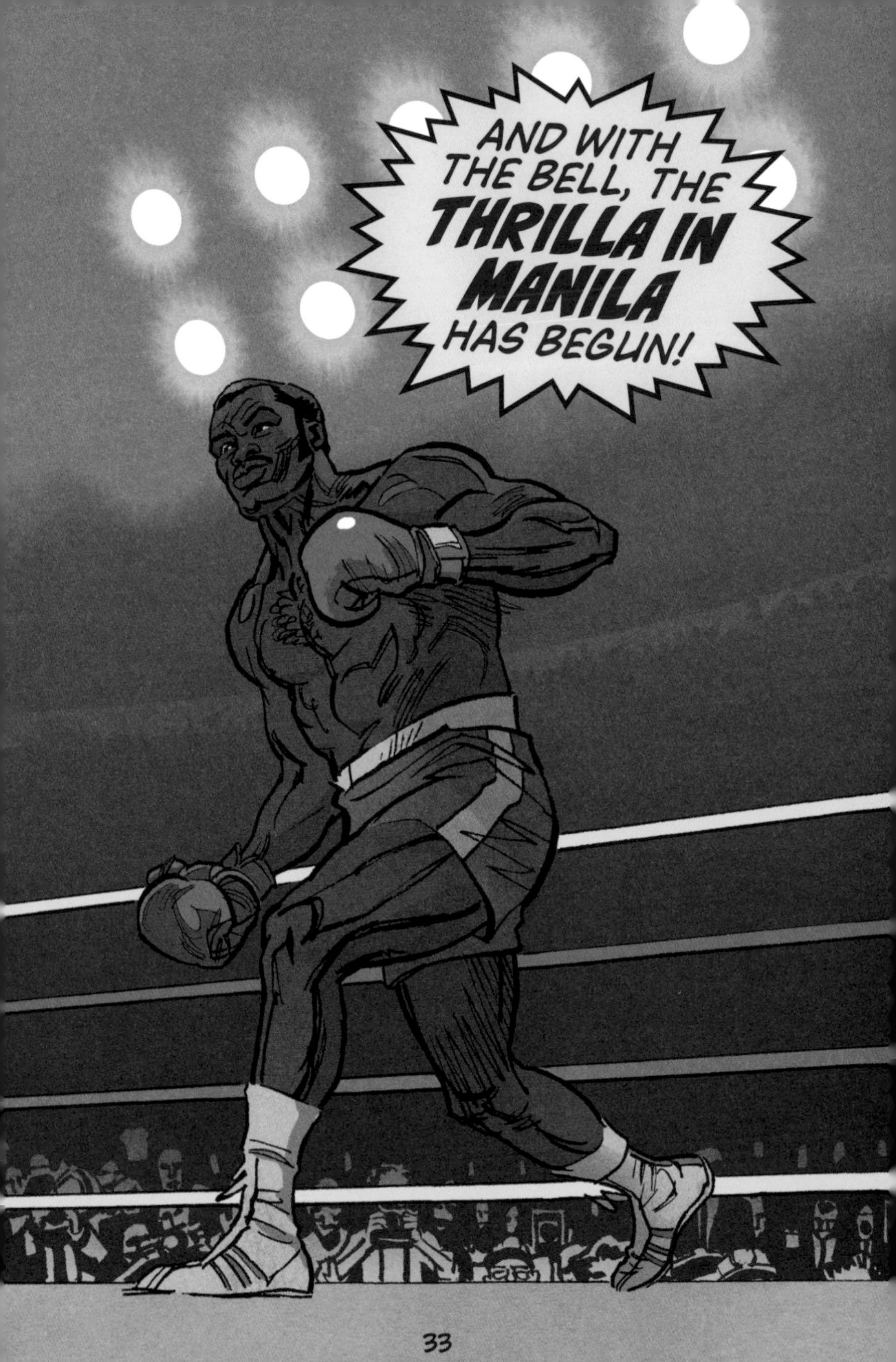
AND WITH THE BELL, THE THRILLA IN MANILA HAS BEGUN!

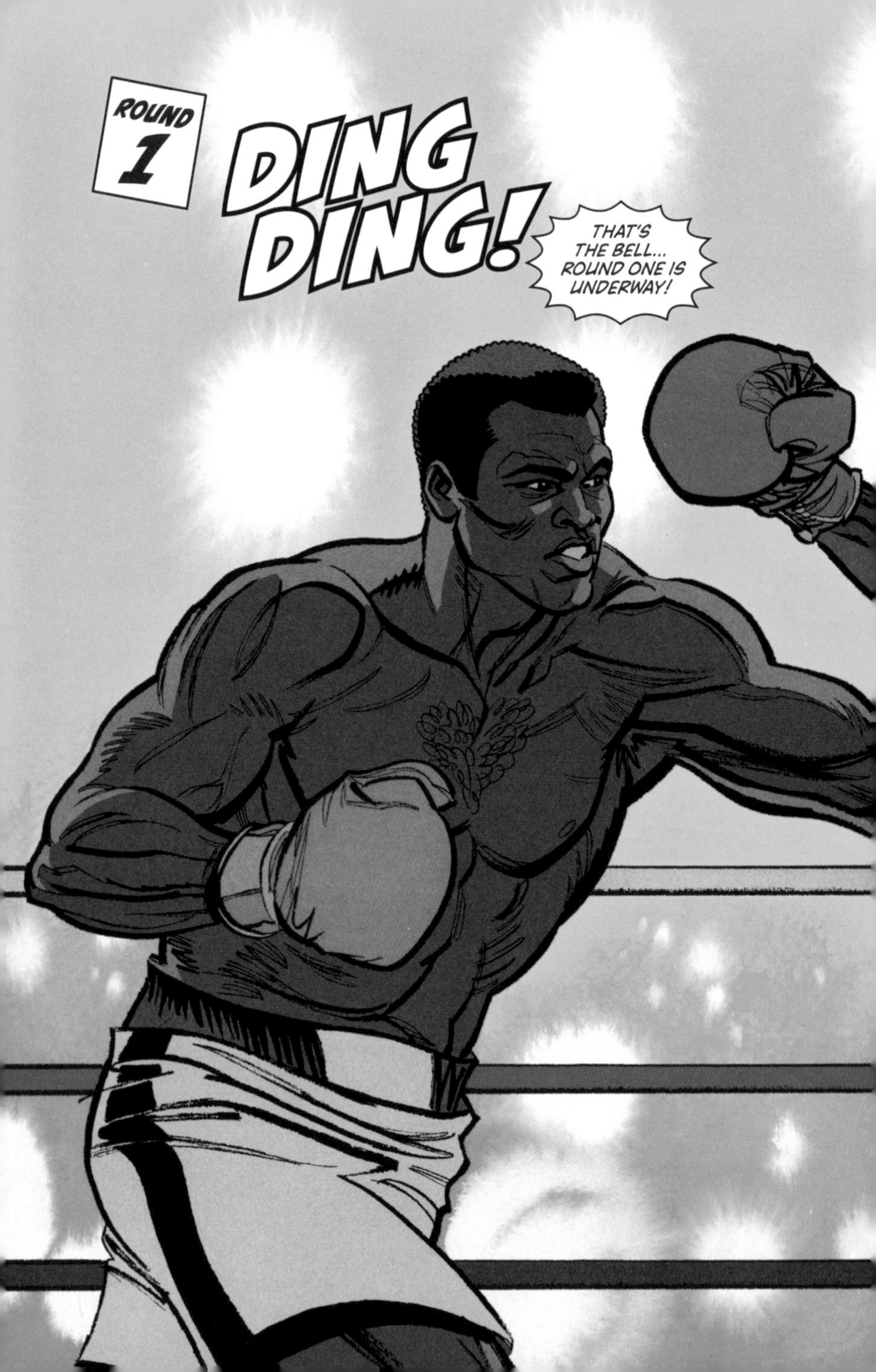
ROUND 1
DING DING!
THAT'S THE BELL... ROUND ONE IS UNDERWAY!

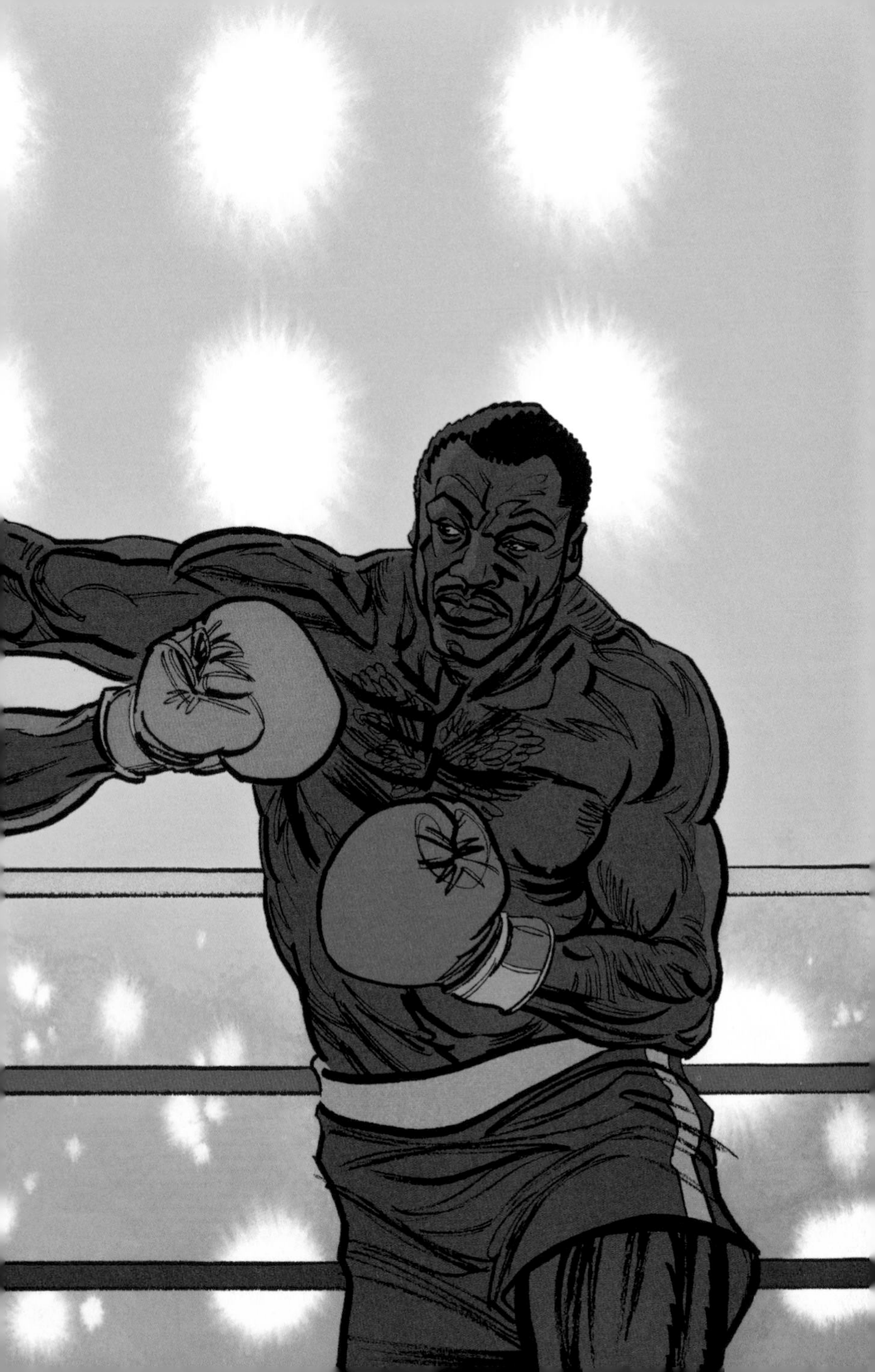

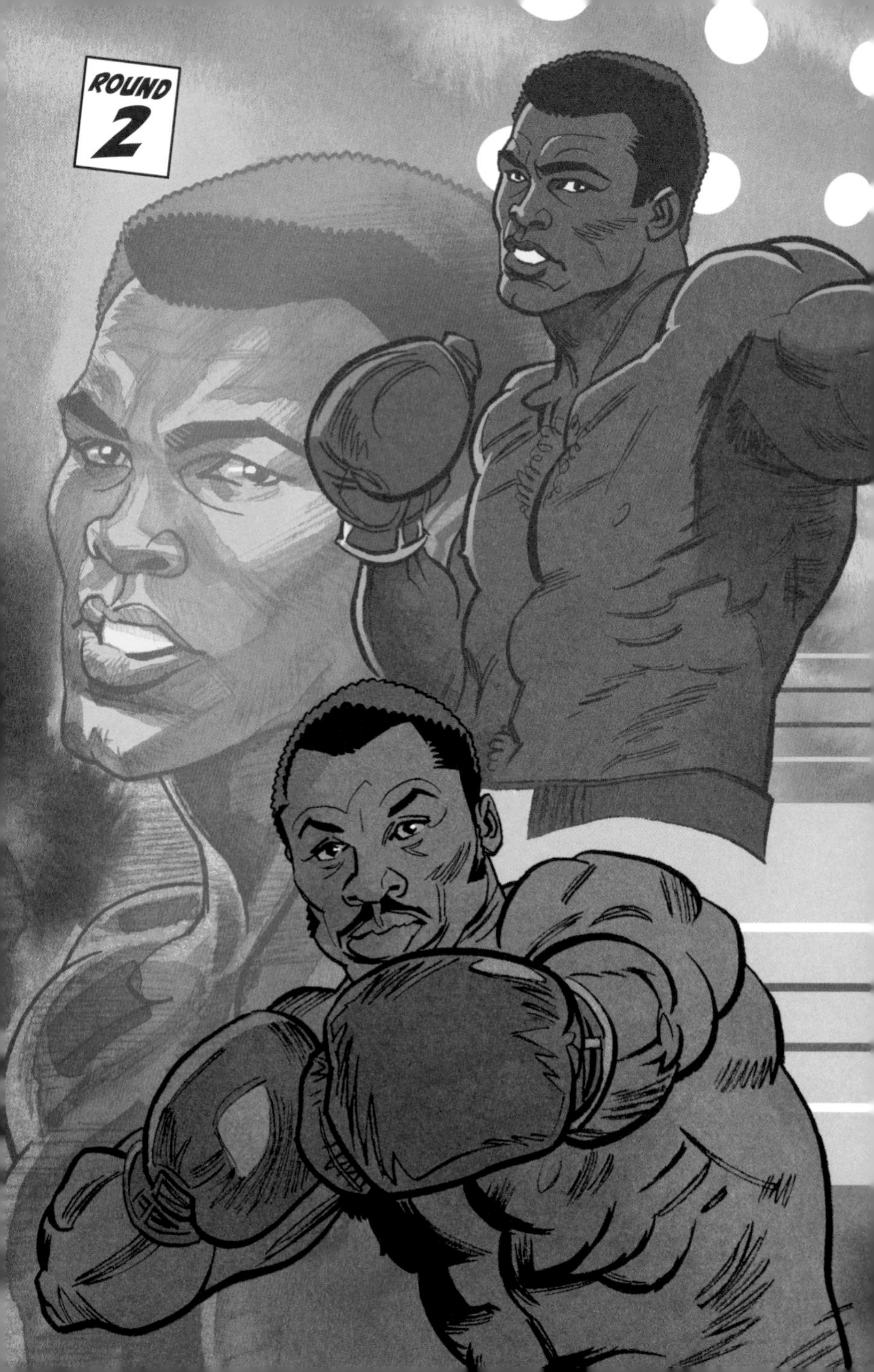
ROUND
2

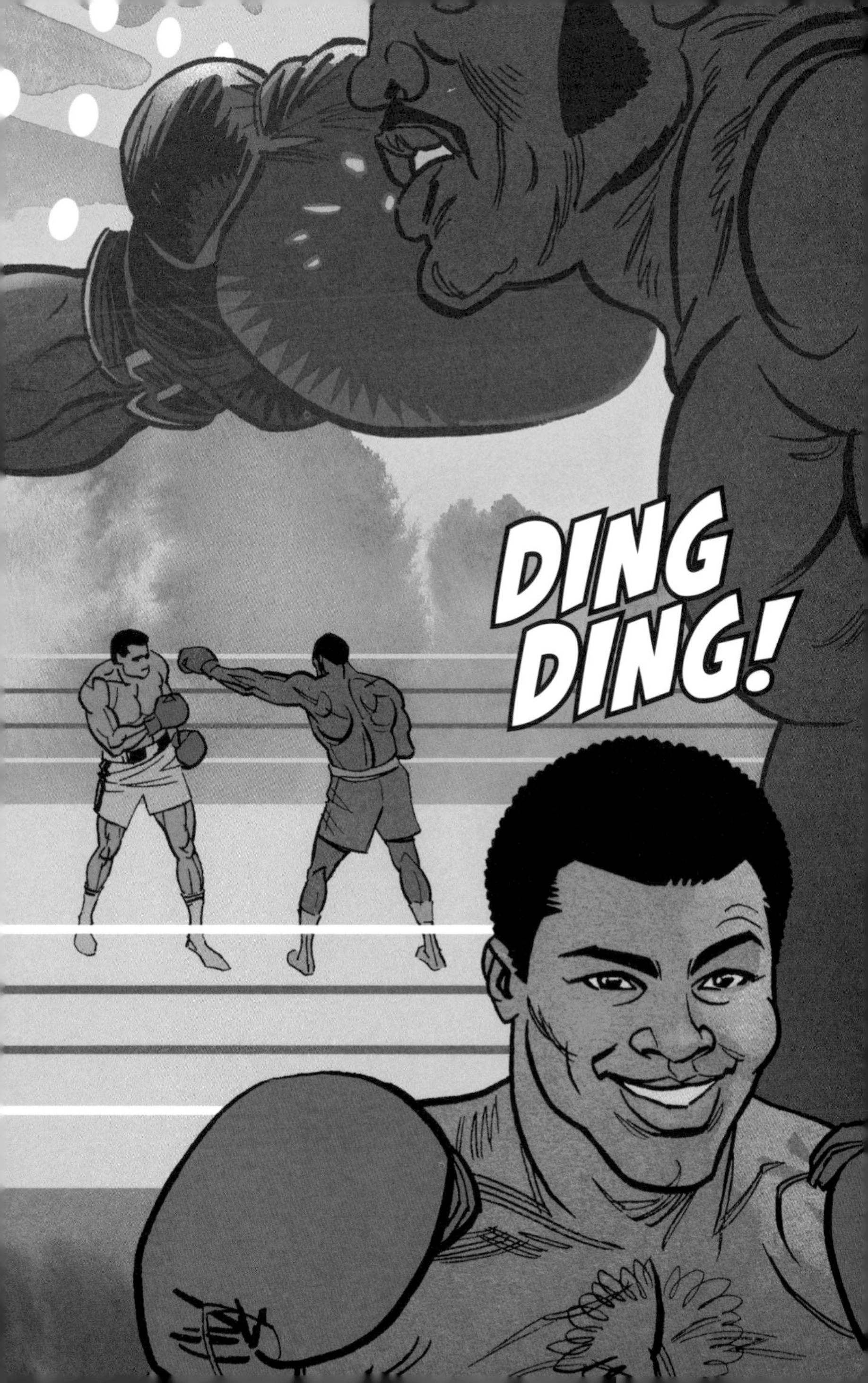
DING DING!

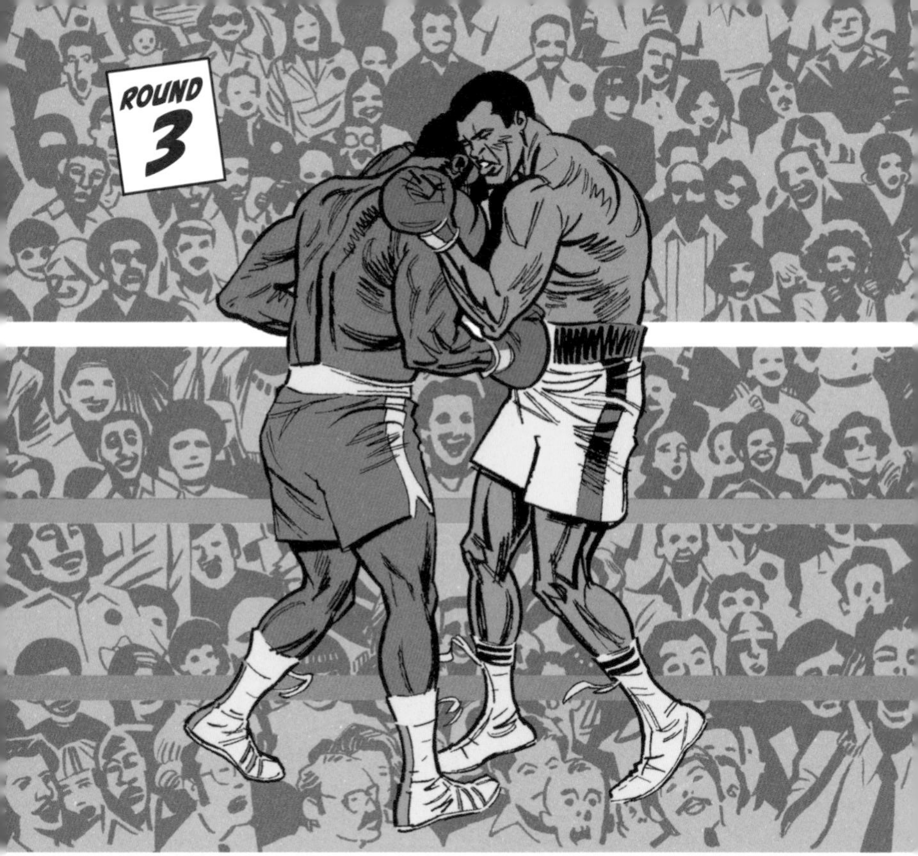
ROUND
3

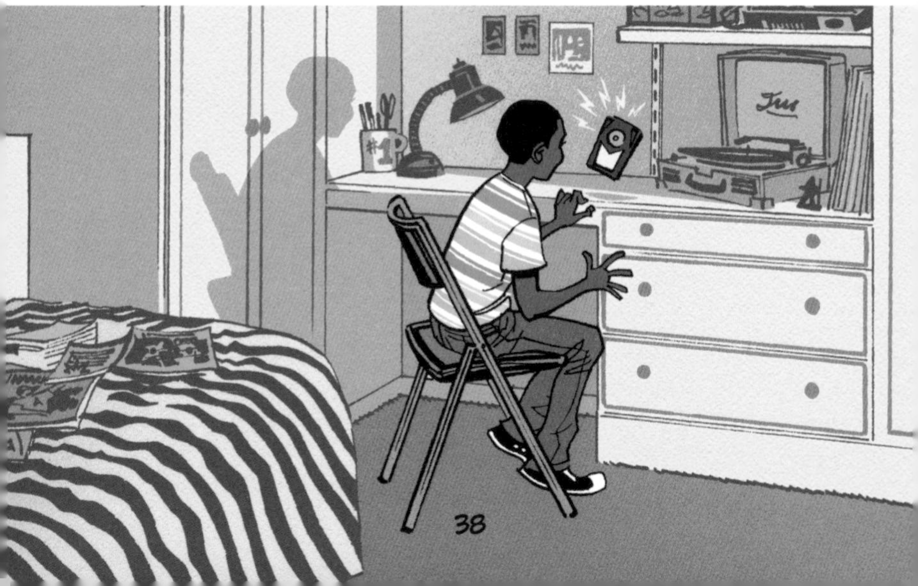

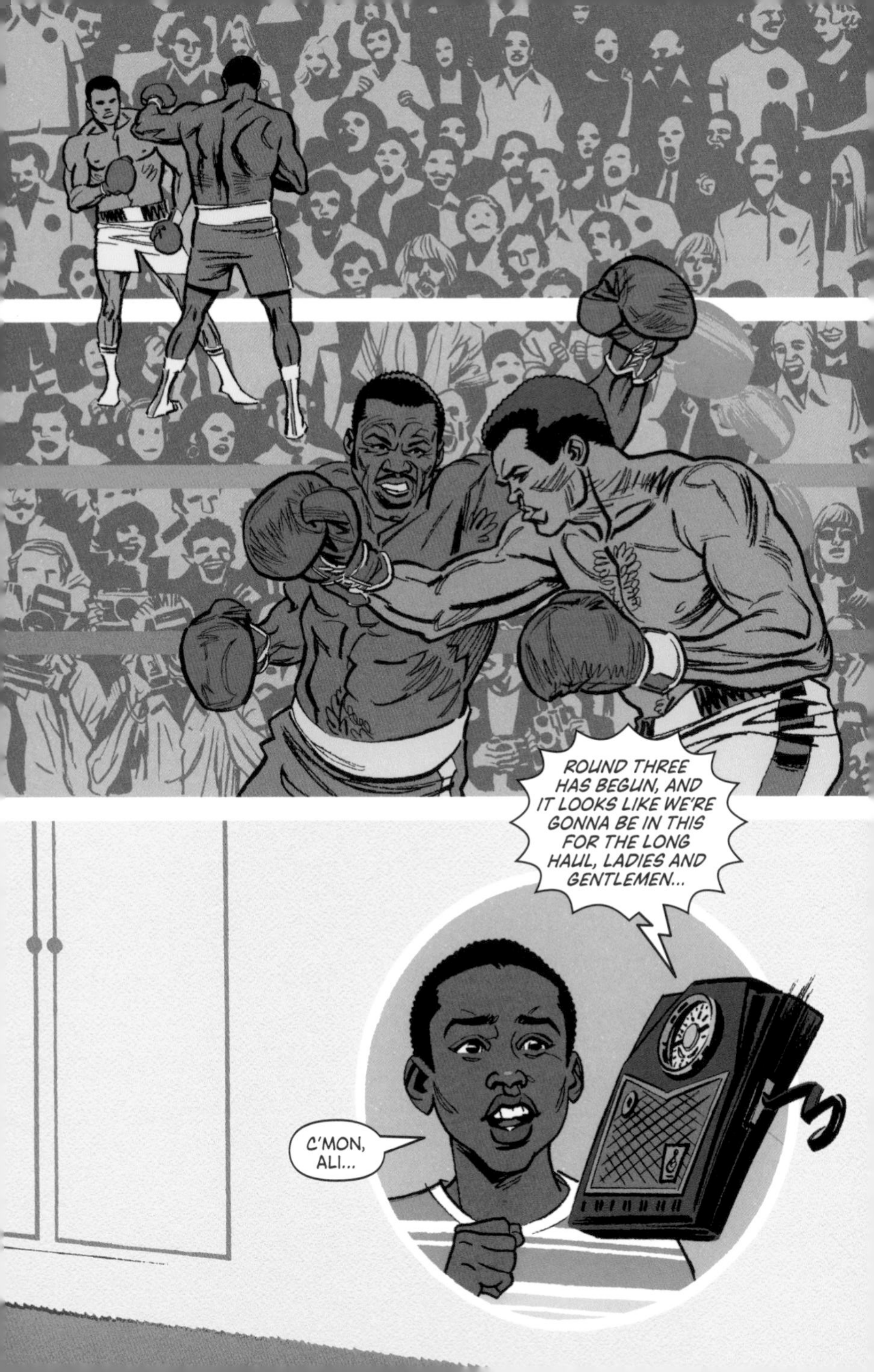
ROUND THREE HAS BEGUN, AND IT LOOKS LIKE WE'RE GONNA BE IN THIS FOR THE LONG HAUL, LADIES AND GENTLEMEN...
C'MON, ALI...

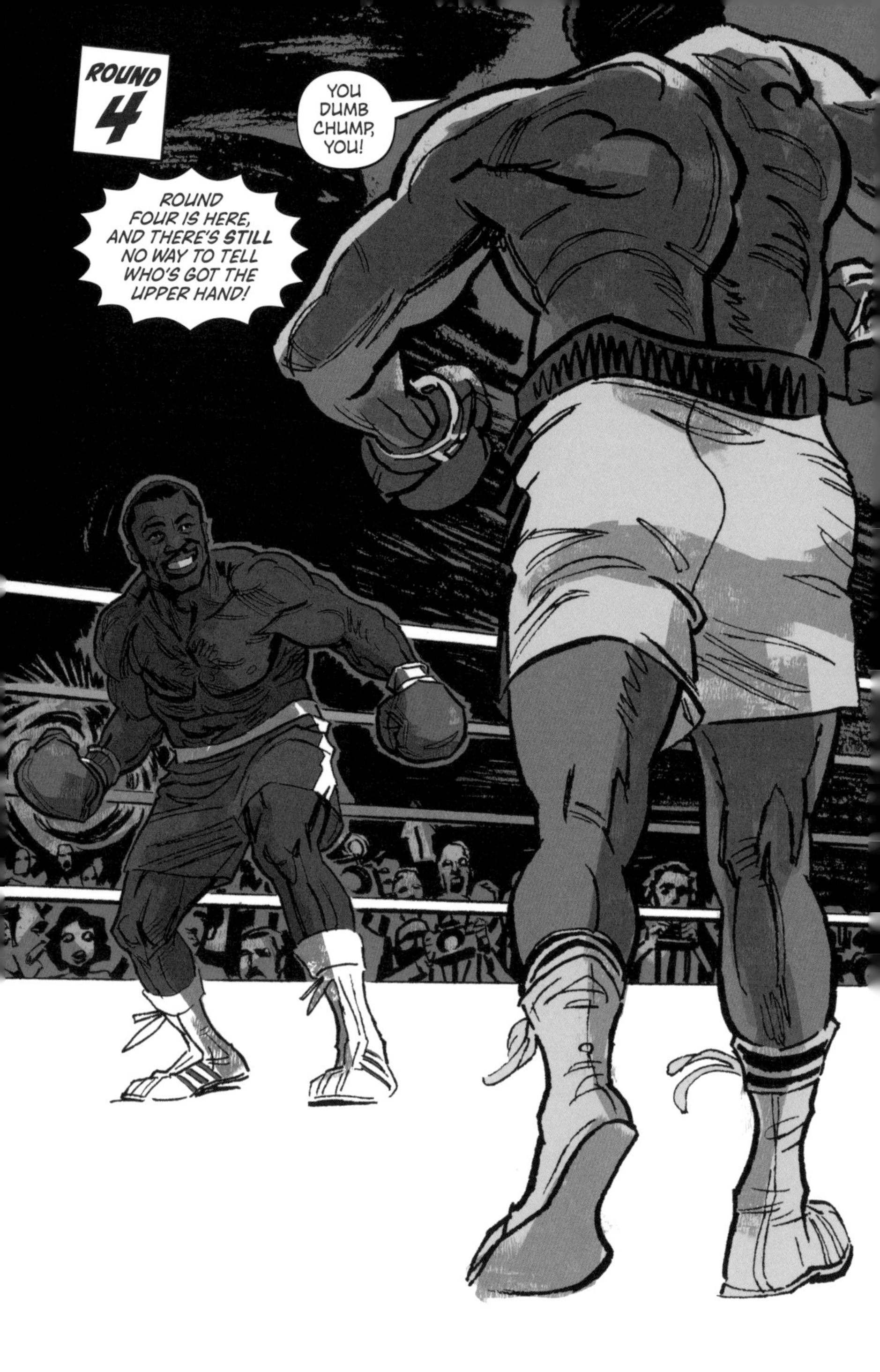
ROUND 4
YOU DUMB CHUMP, YOU!
ROUND FOUR IS HERE, AND THERE'S STILL NO WAY TO TELL WHO'S GOT THE UPPER HAND!

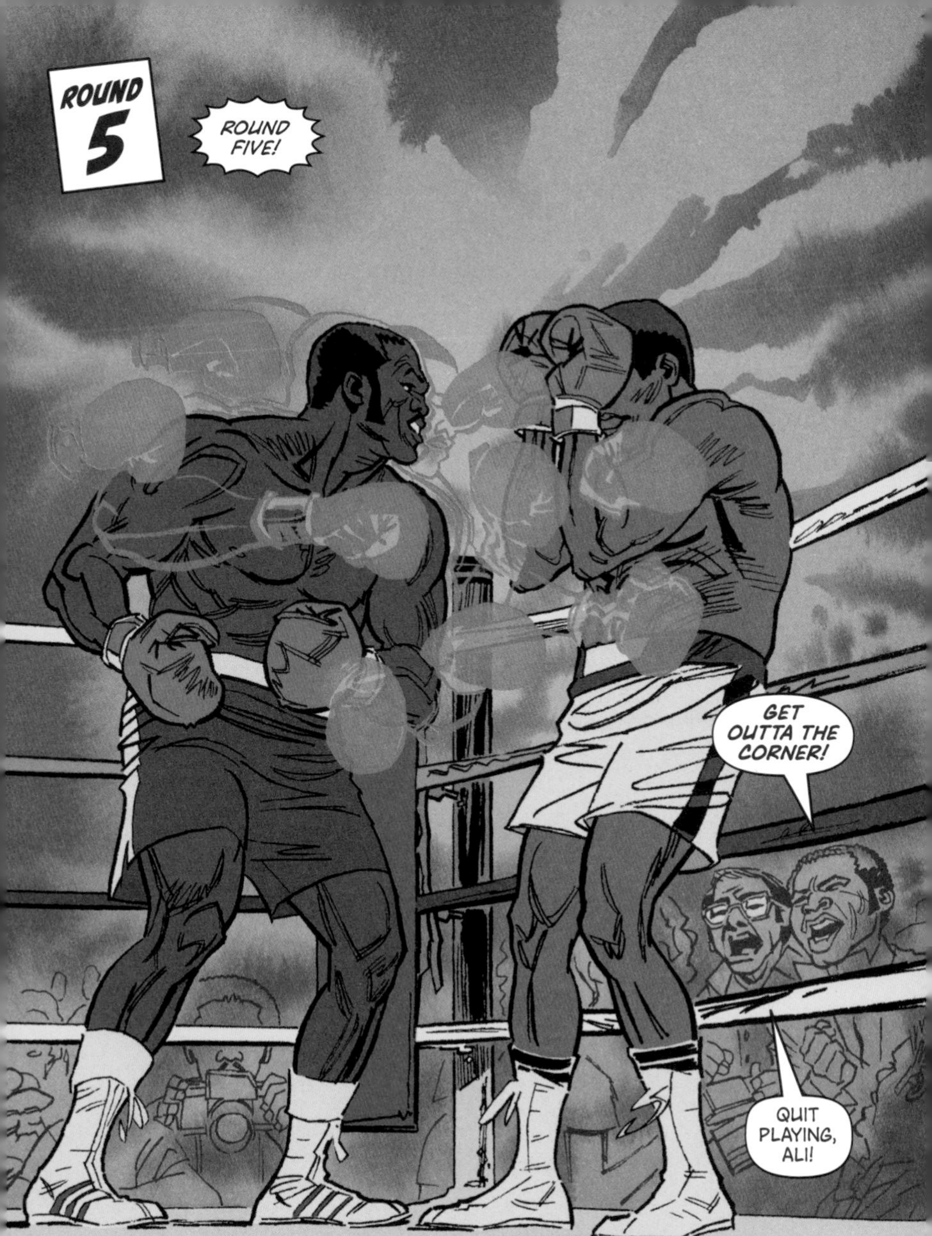
ROUND
5
ROUND FIVE!
GET OUTTA THE CORNER!
QUIT PLAYING, ALI!

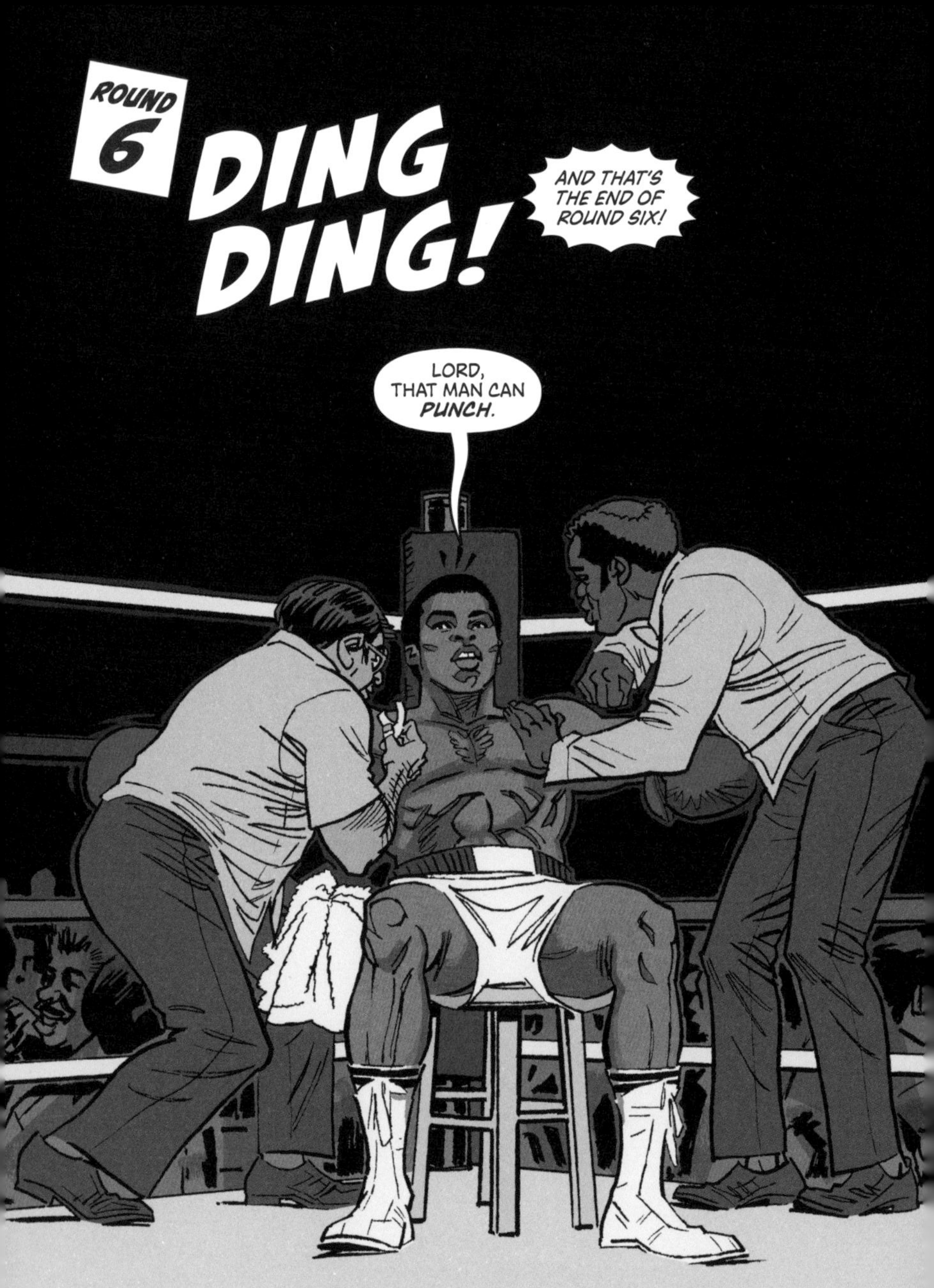
ROUND
6
DING DING!
AND THAT'S THE END OF ROUND SIX!
LORD, THAT MAN CAN PUNCH.

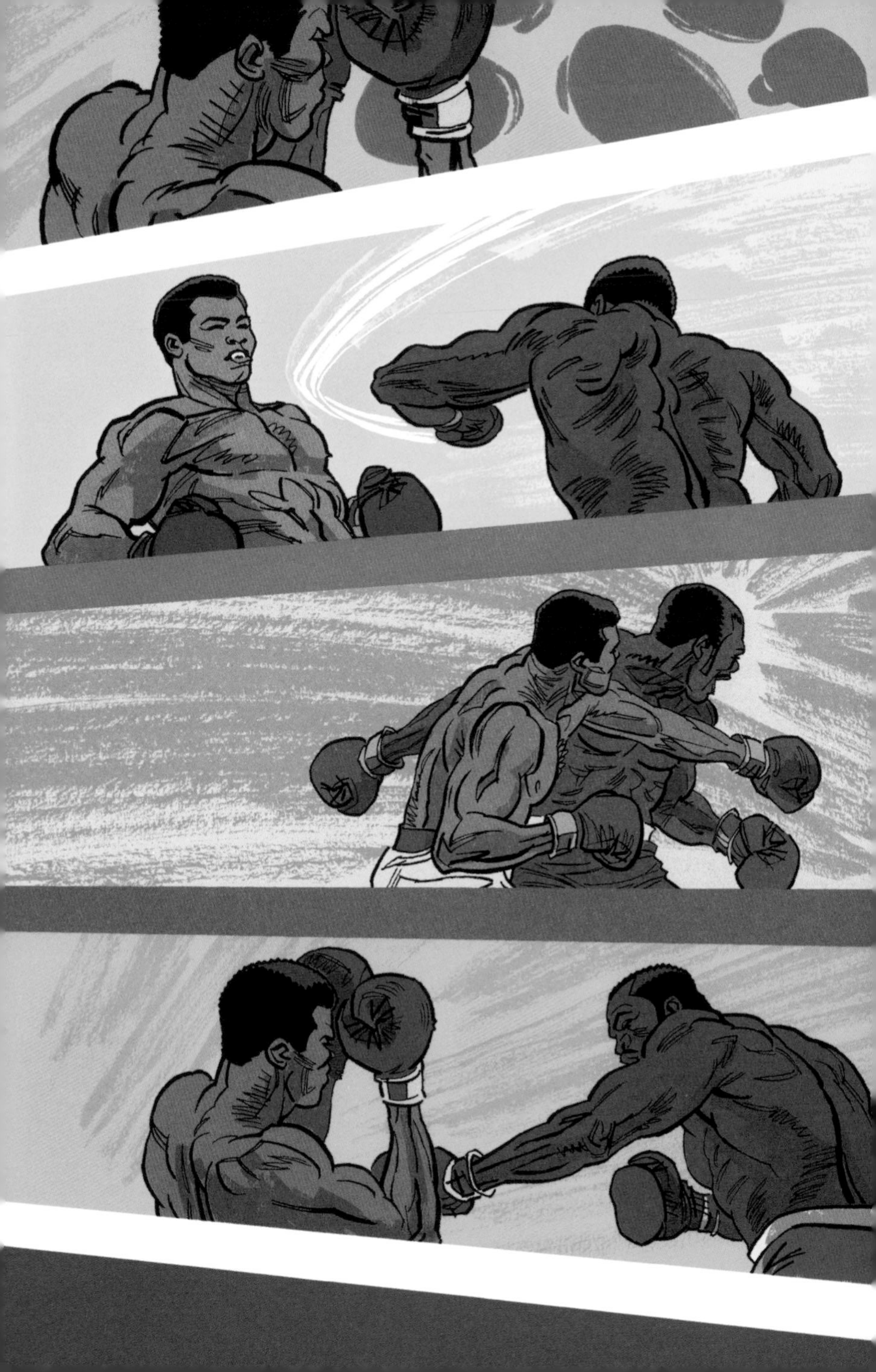

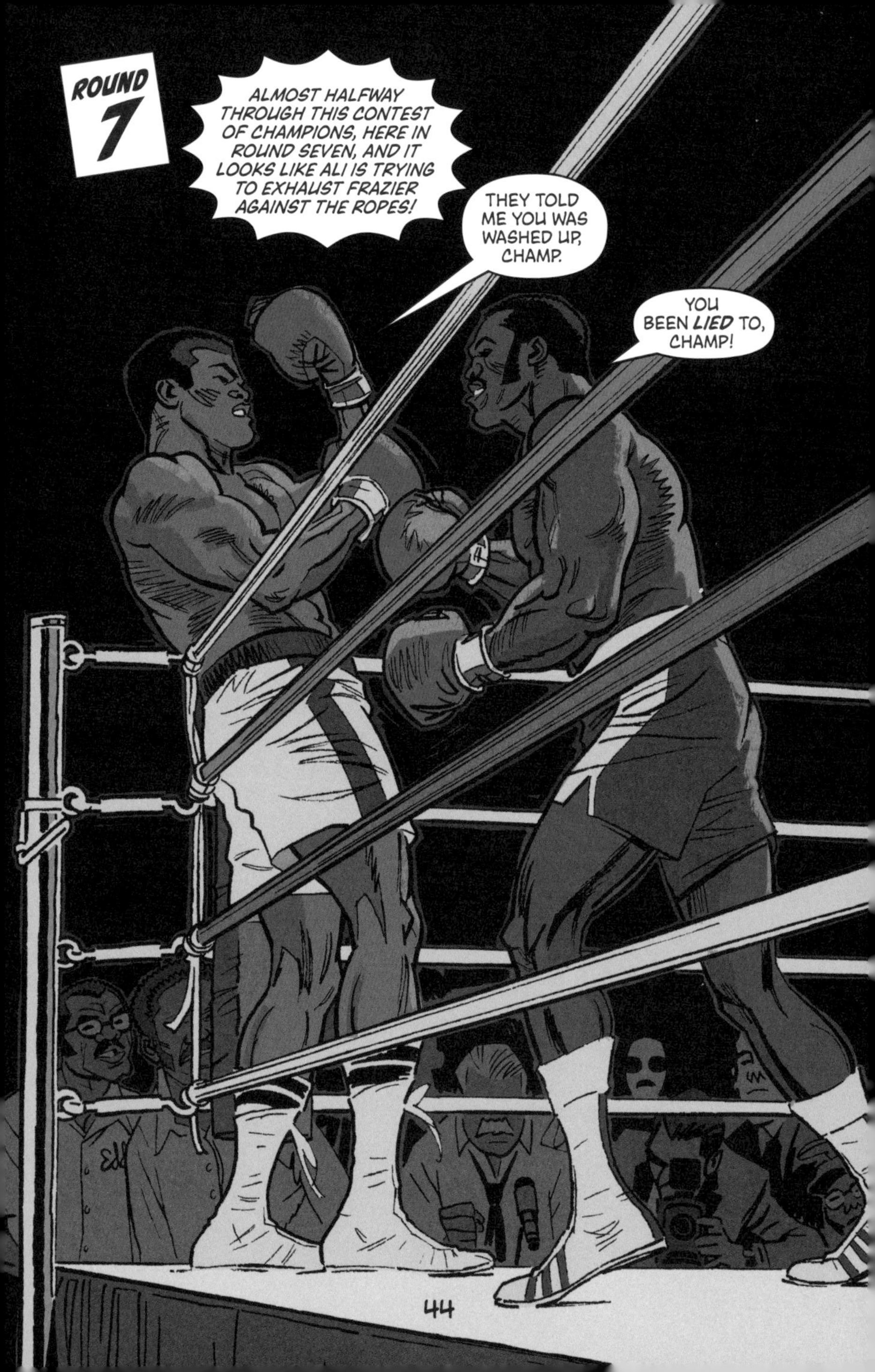
ROUND 7
ALMOST HALFWAY THROUGH THIS CONTEST OF CHAMPIONS, HERE IN ROUND SEVEN, AND IT LOOKS LIKE ALI IS TRYING TO EXHAUST FRAZIER AGAINST THE ROPES!
THEY TOLD ME YOU WAS WASHED UP, CHAMP.
YOU BEEN *LIED* TO, CHAMP!

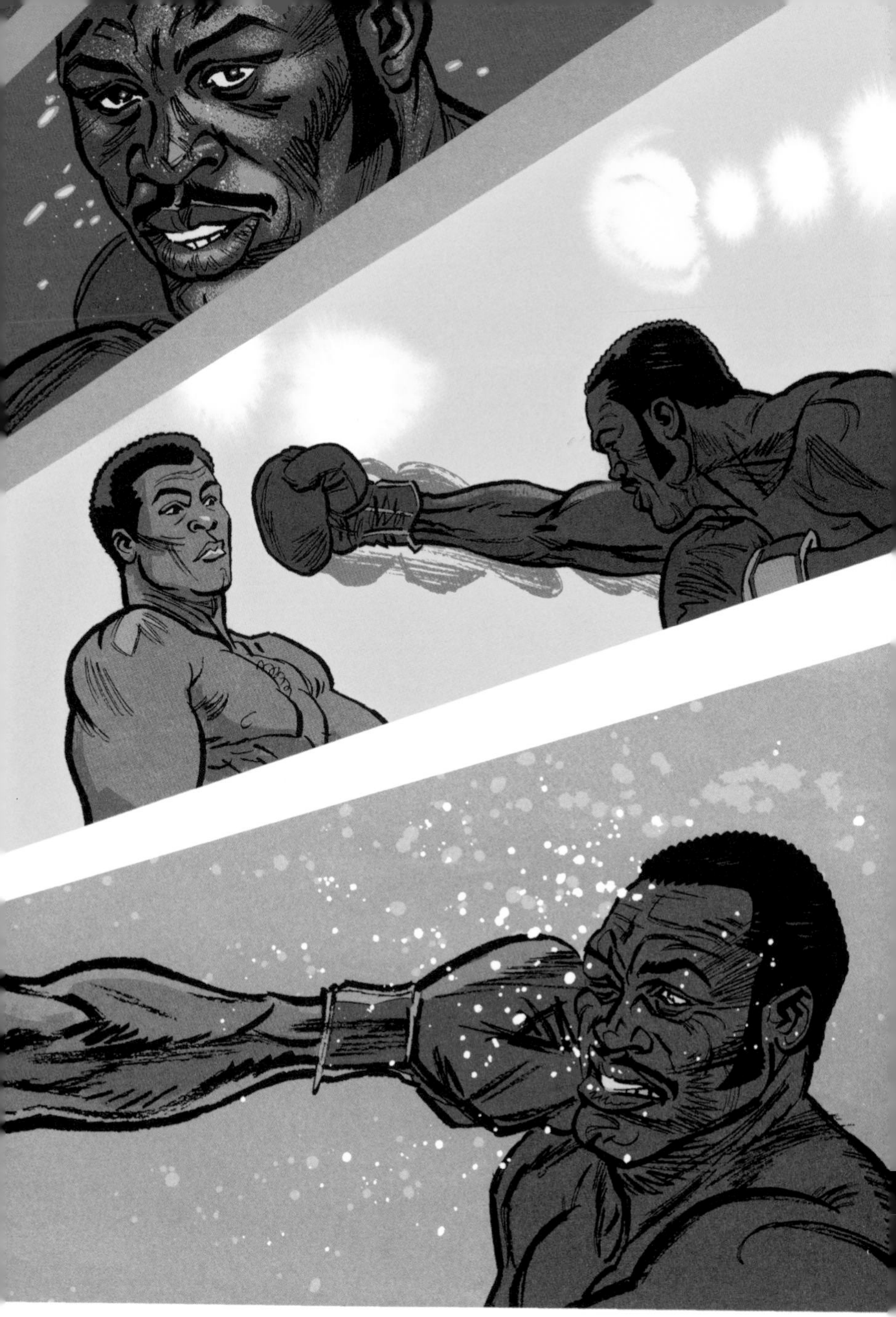

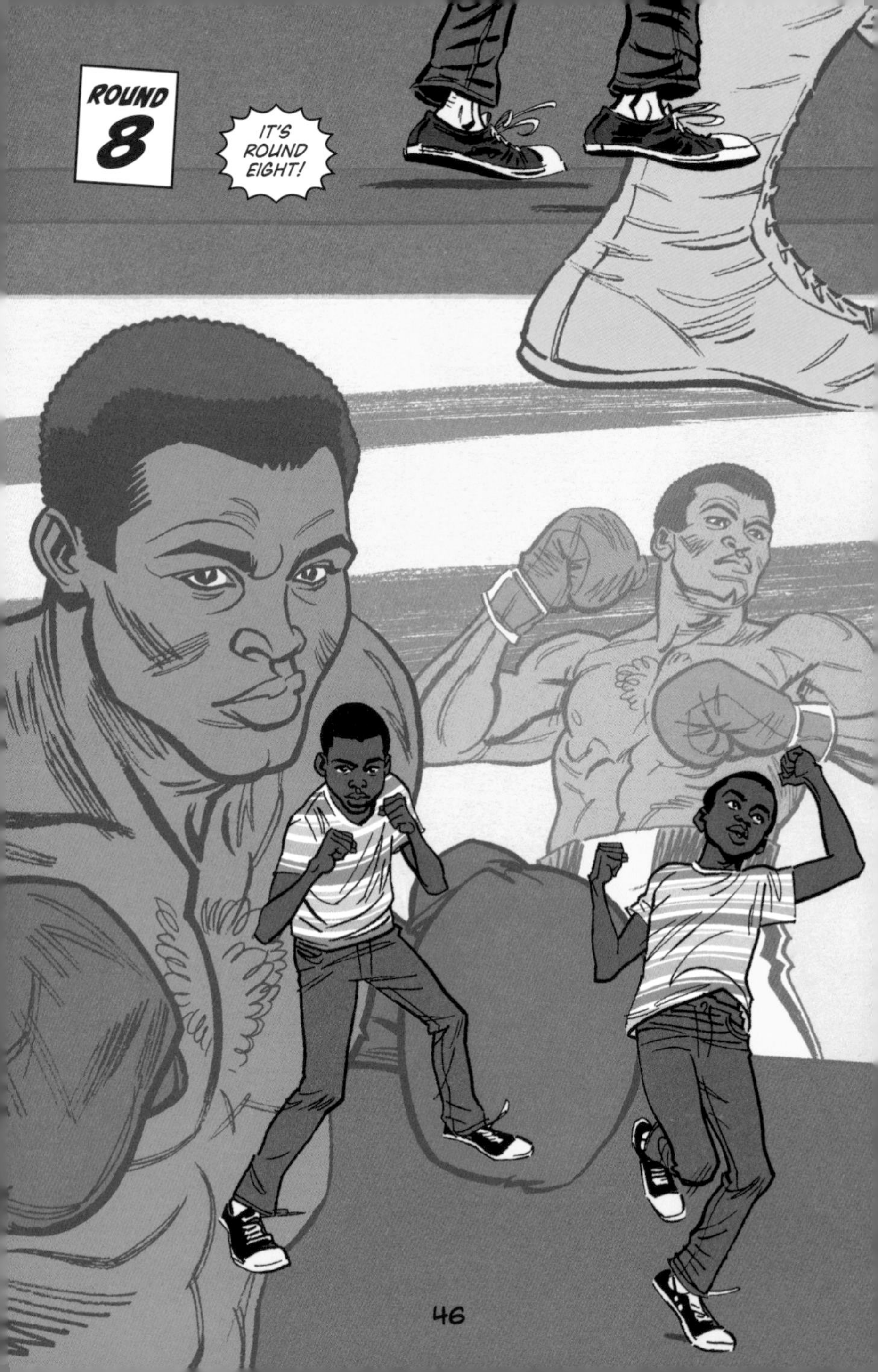
ROUND
8
IT'S
ROUND
EIGHT!

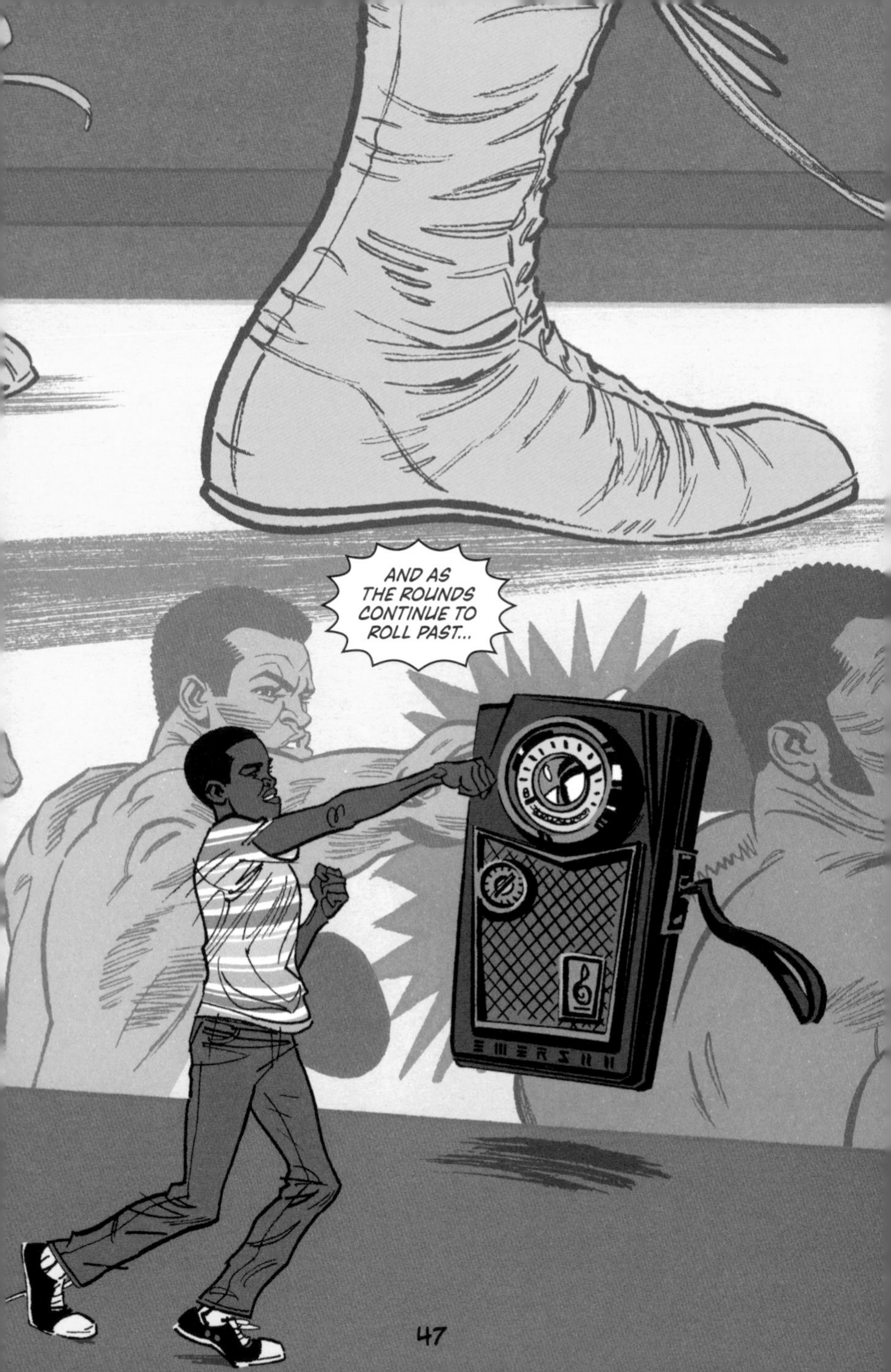
AND AS
THE ROUNDS
CONTINUE TO
ROLL PAST...

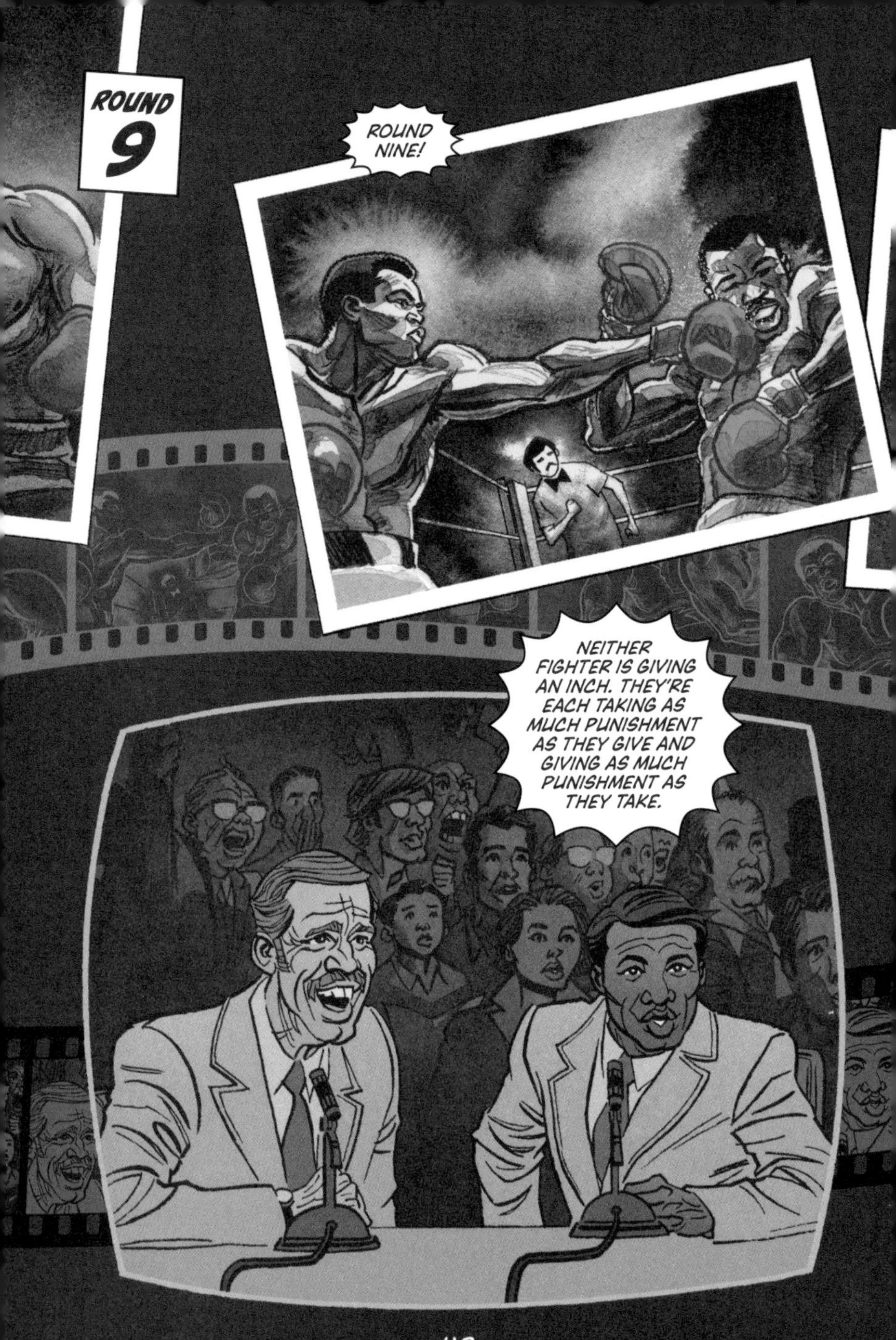
ROUND 9
ROUND NINE!
NEITHER FIGHTER IS GIVING AN INCH. THEY'RE EACH TAKING AS MUCH PUNISHMENT AS THEY GIVE AND GIVING AS MUCH PUNISHMENT AS THEY TAKE.

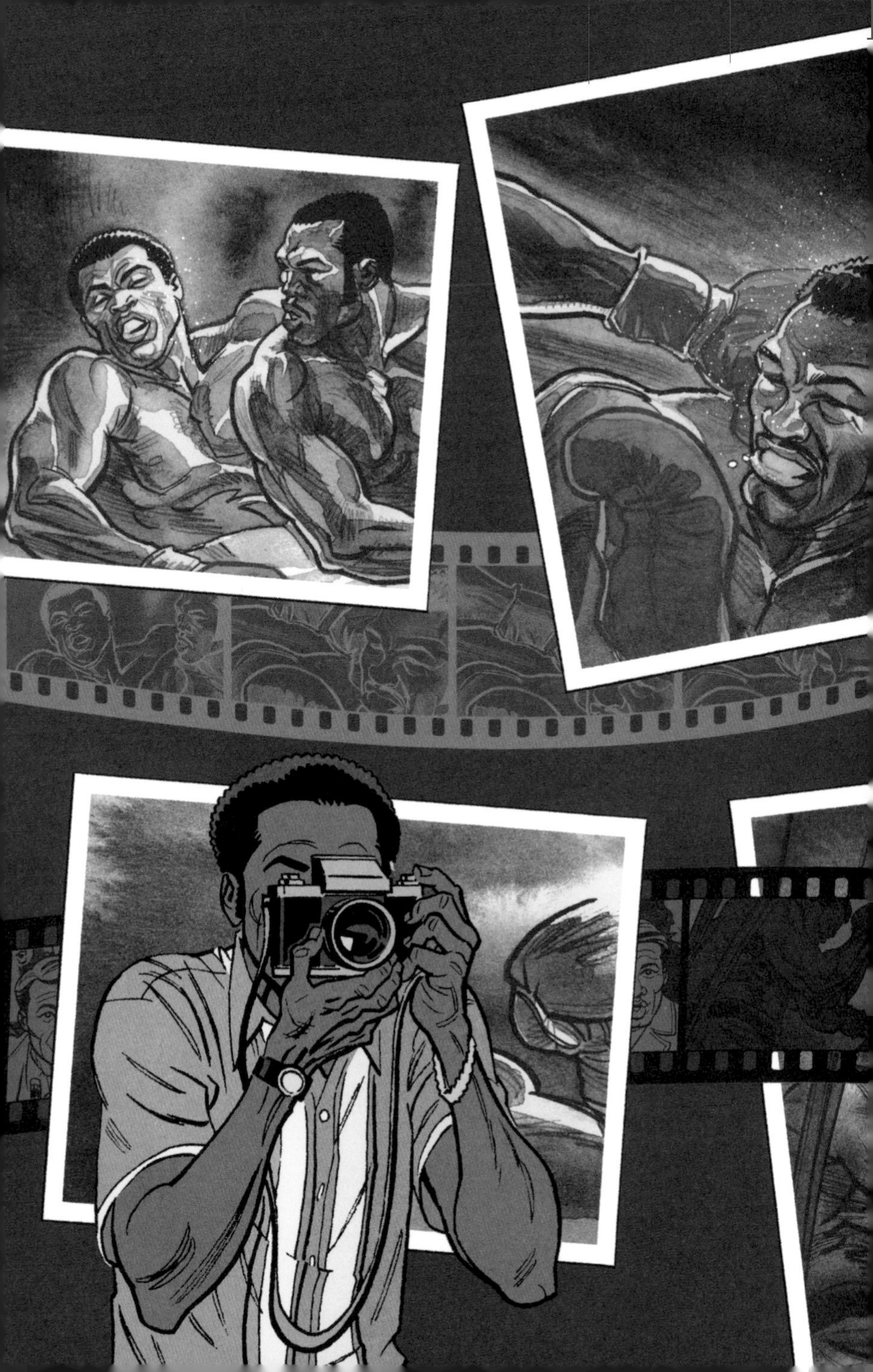

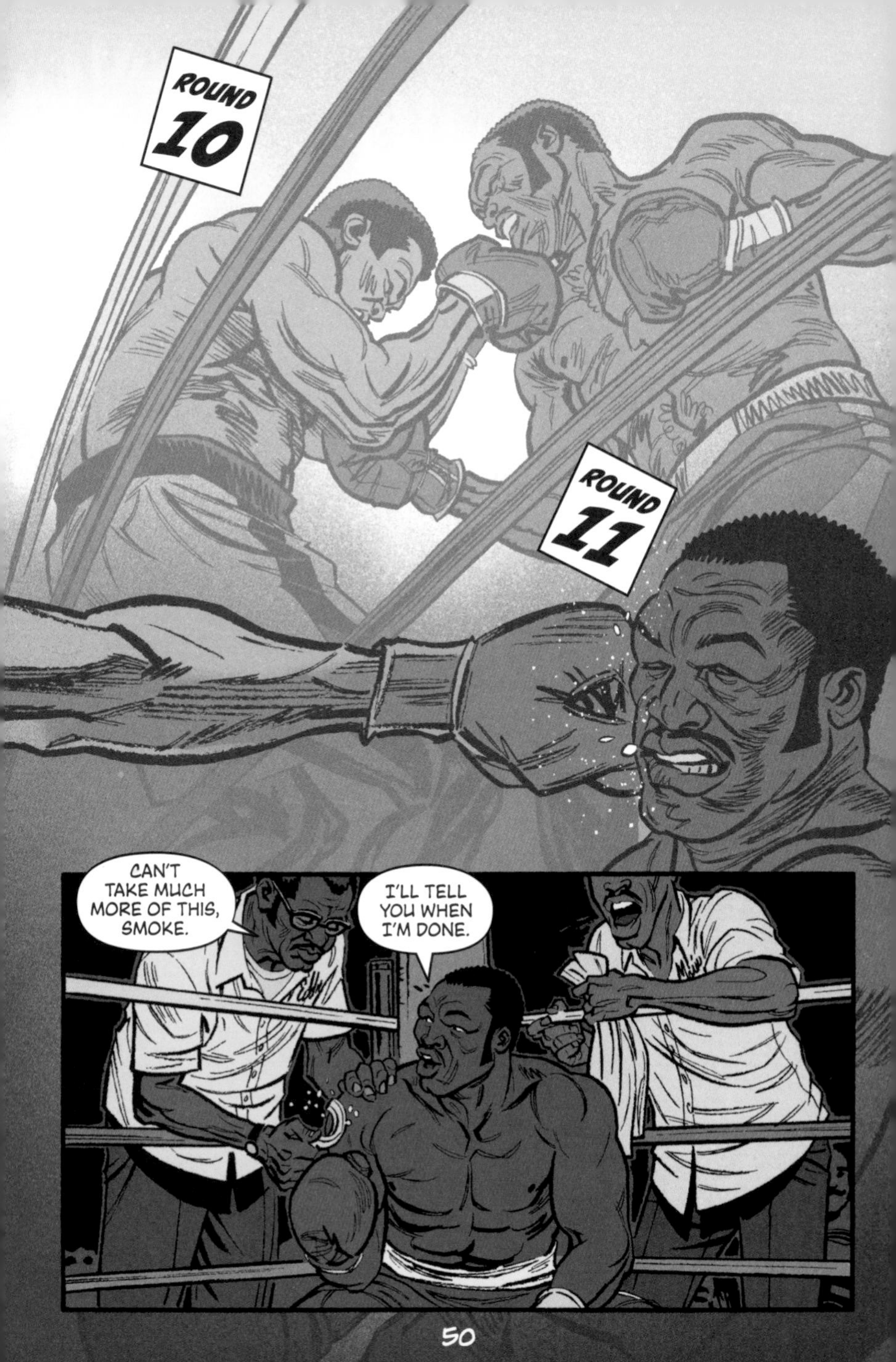

ROUND 10
ROUND 11
CAN'T TAKE MUCH MORE OF THIS, SMOKE.
I'LL TELL YOU WHEN I'M DONE.

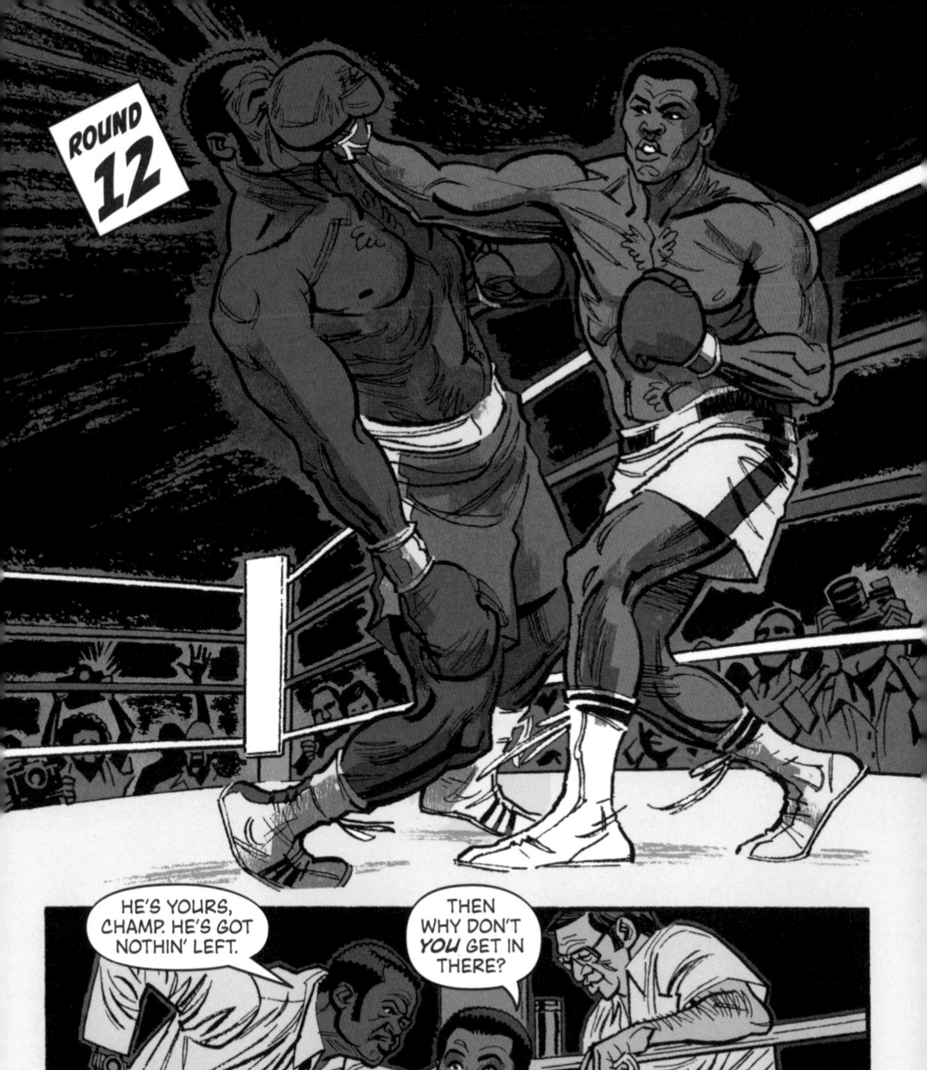
ROUND 12

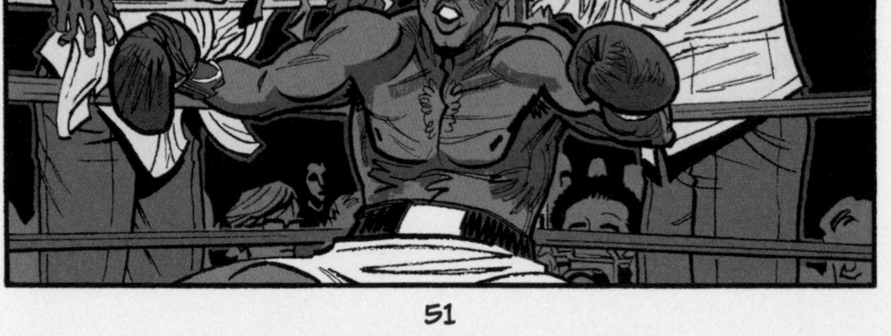
HE'S YOURS, CHAMP. HE'S GOT NOTHIN' LEFT.
THEN WHY DON'T *YOU* GET IN THERE?

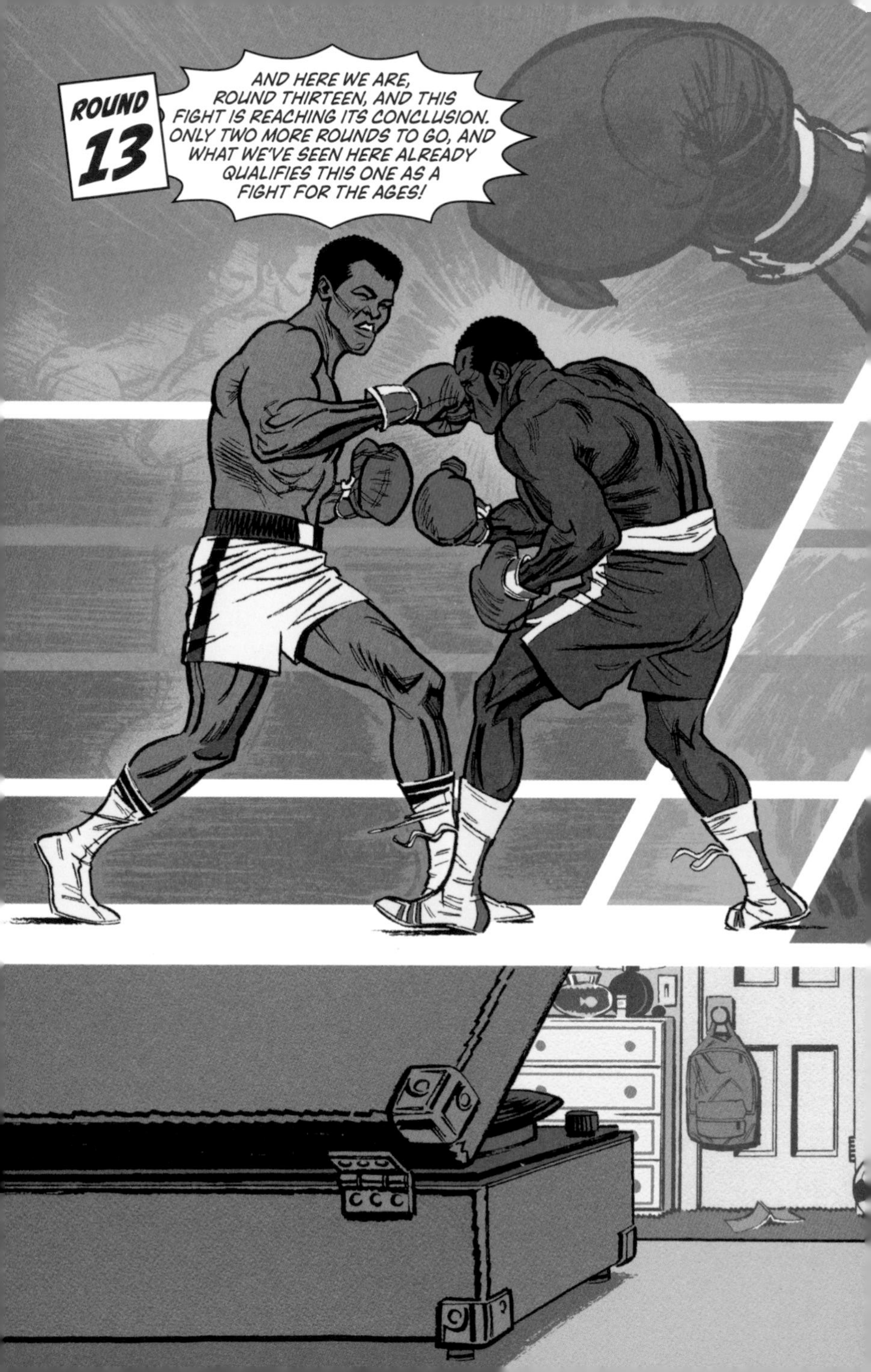
ROUND 13
AND HERE WE ARE, ROUND THIRTEEN, AND THIS FIGHT IS REACHING ITS CONCLUSION. ONLY TWO MORE ROUNDS TO GO, AND WHAT WE'VE SEEN HERE ALREADY QUALIFIES THIS ONE AS A FIGHT FOR THE AGES!

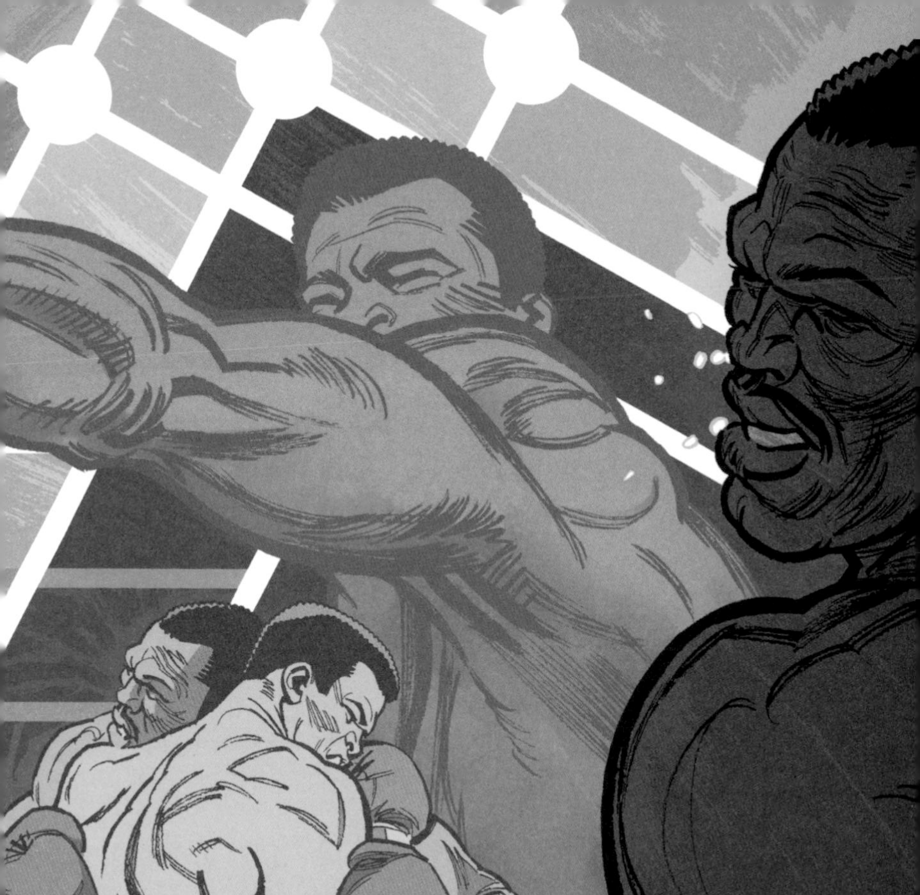

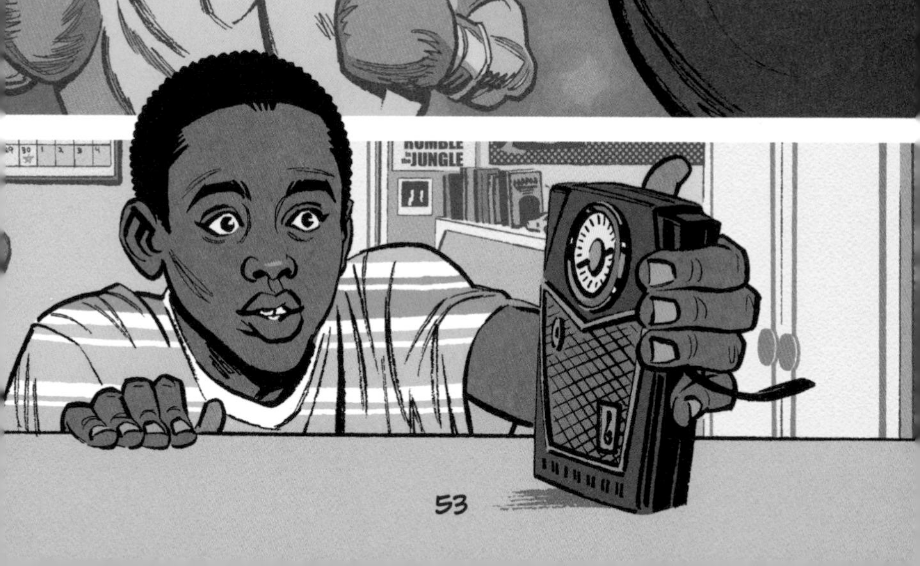
RUMBLE in the JUNGLE

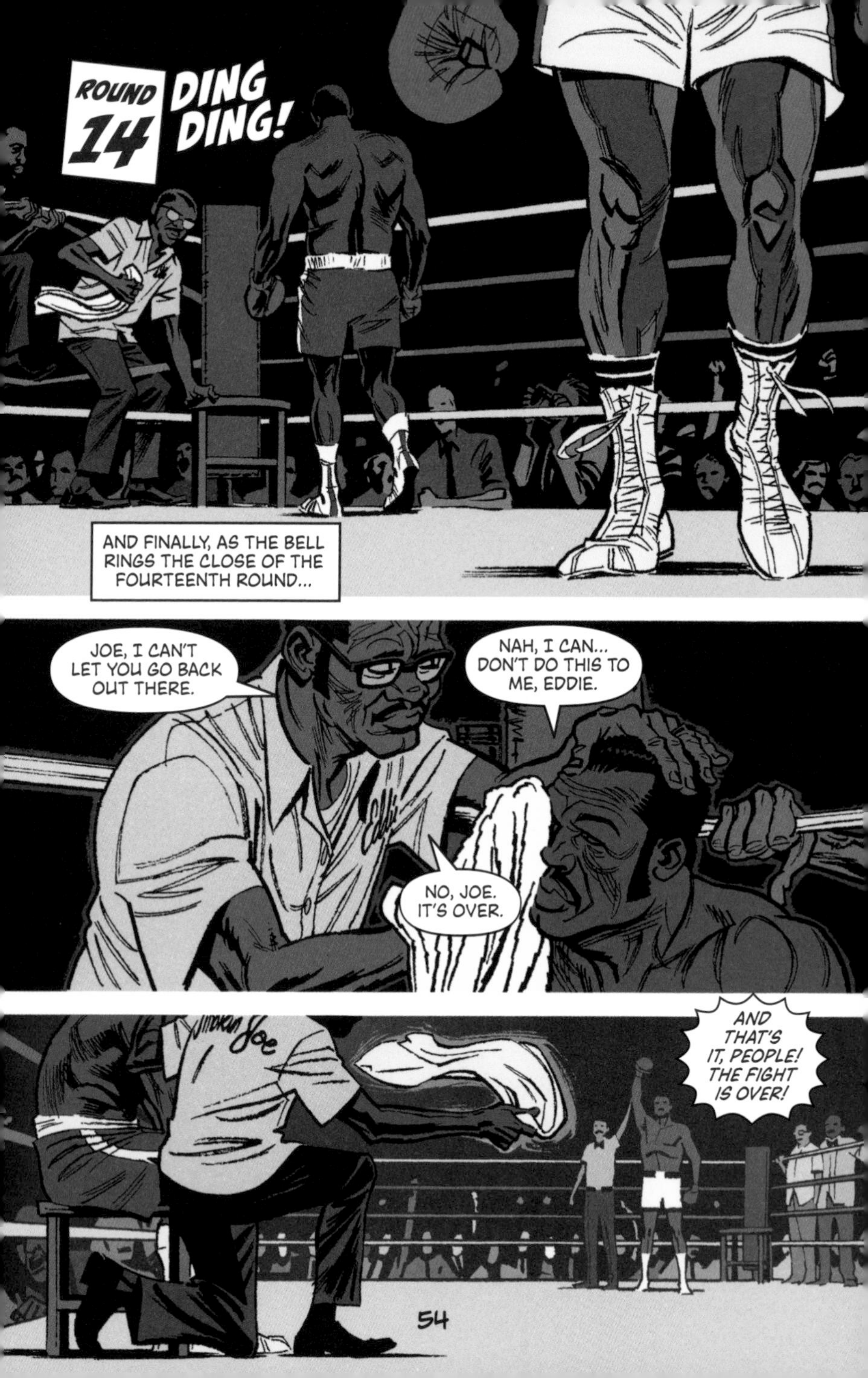
ROUND 14
DING DING!
AND FINALLY, AS THE BELL RINGS THE CLOSE OF THE FOURTEENTH ROUND...
JOE, I CAN'T LET YOU GO BACK OUT THERE.
NAH, I CAN... DON'T DO THIS TO ME, EDDIE.
NO, JOE. IT'S OVER.
AND THAT'S IT, PEOPLE! THE FIGHT IS OVER!

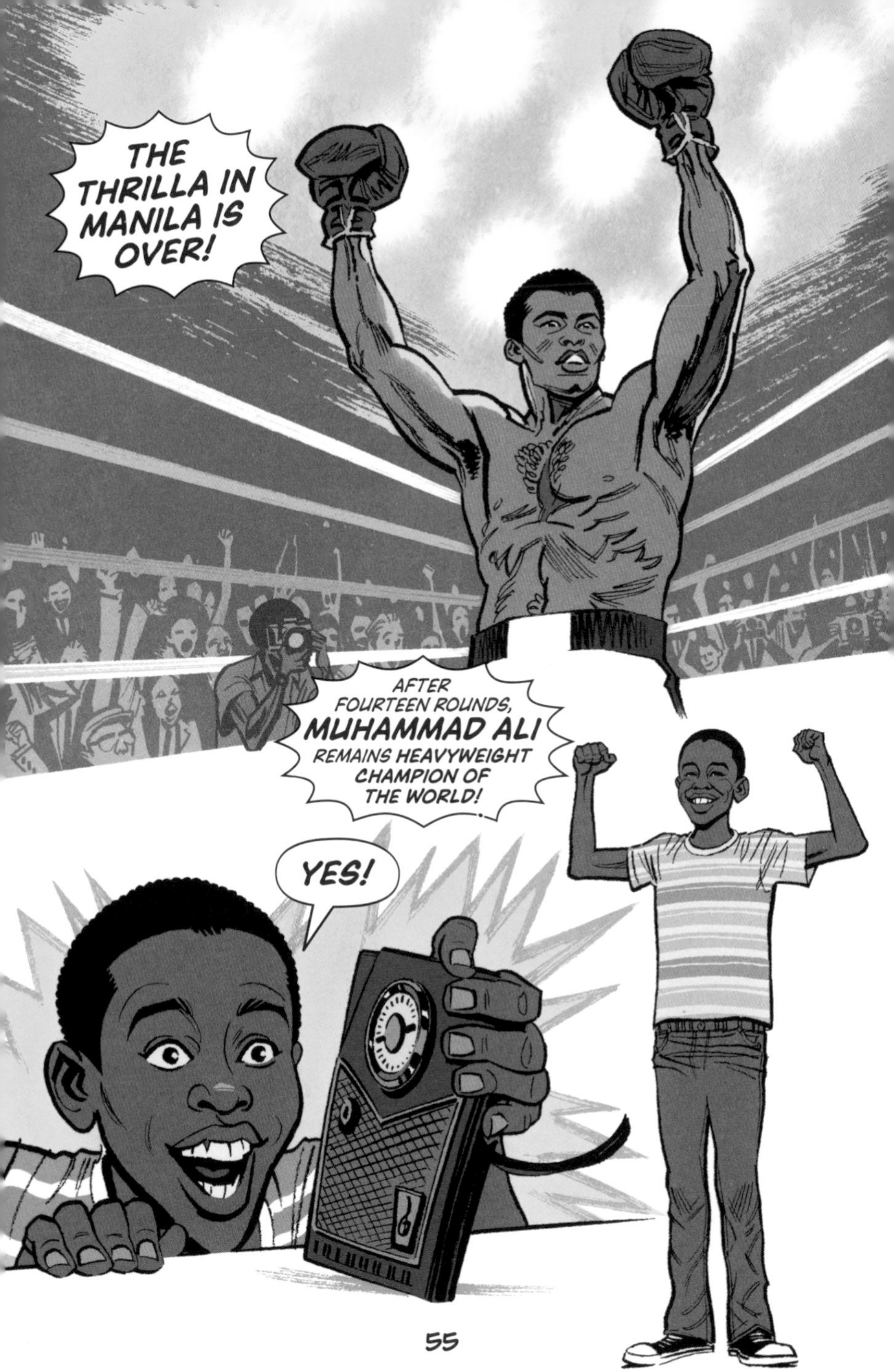
THE THRILLA IN MANILA IS OVER!
AFTER FOURTEEN ROUNDS, MUHAMMAD ALI REMAINS HEAVYWEIGHT CHAMPION OF THE WORLD!
YES!

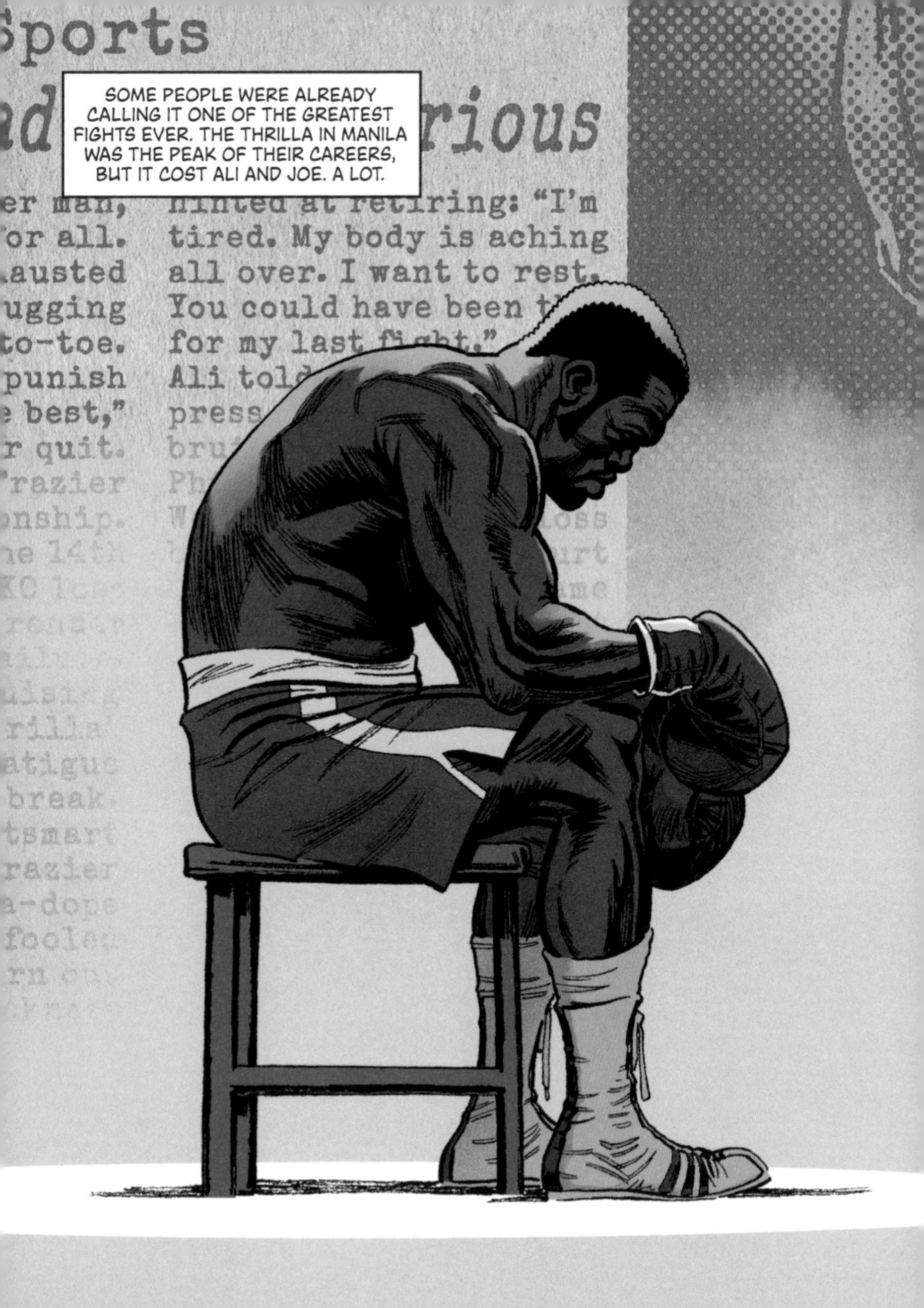
SOME PEOPLE WERE ALREADY CALLING IT ONE OF THE GREATEST FIGHTS EVER. THE THRILLA IN MANILA WAS THE PEAK OF THEIR CAREERS, BUT IT COST ALI AND JOE. A LOT.

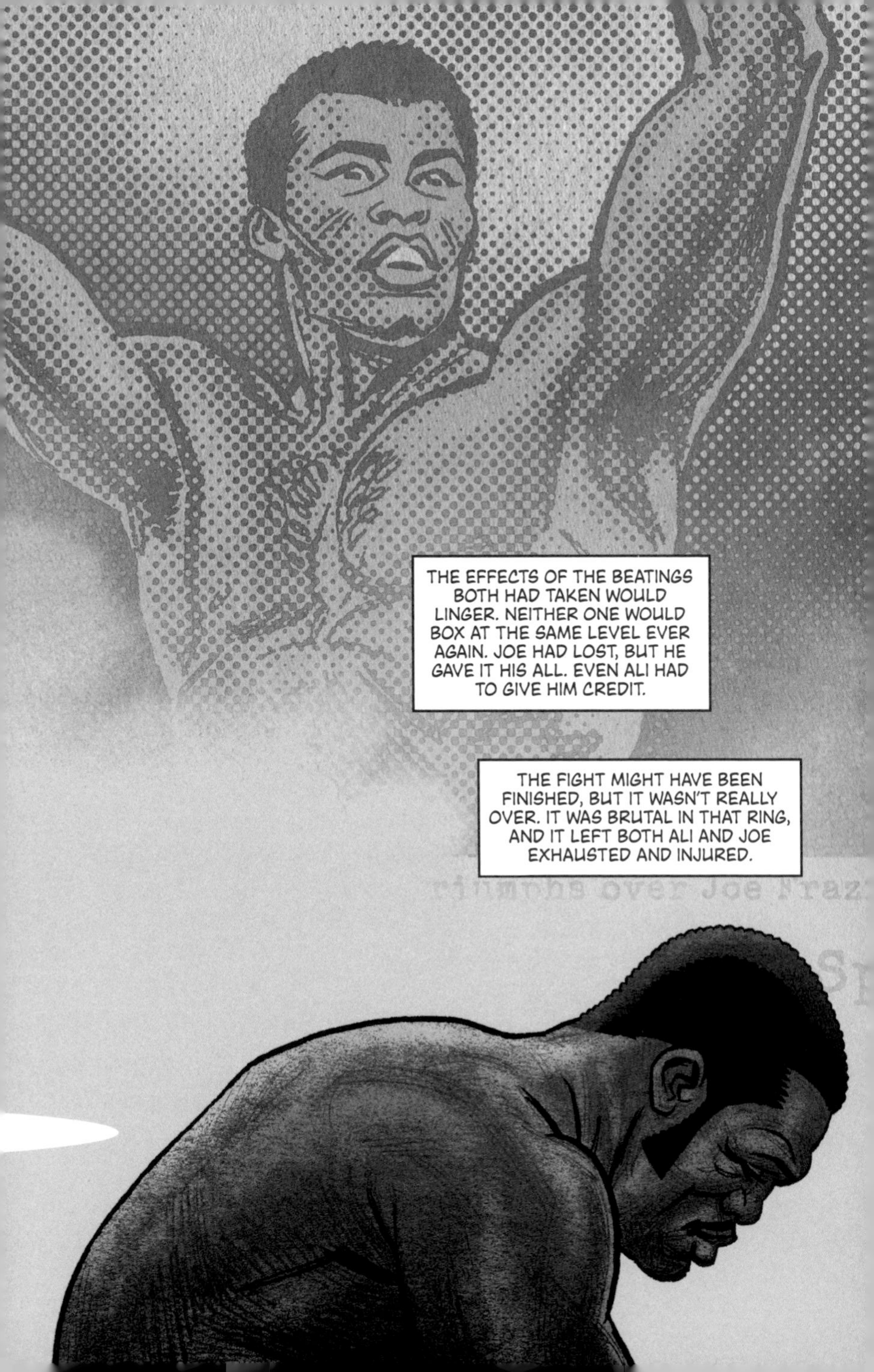
THE EFFECTS OF THE BEATINGS BOTH HAD TAKEN WOULD LINGER. NEITHER ONE WOULD BOX AT THE SAME LEVEL EVER AGAIN. JOE HAD LOST, BUT HE GAVE IT HIS ALL. EVEN ALI HAD TO GIVE HIM CREDIT.
THE FIGHT MIGHT HAVE BEEN FINISHED, BUT IT WASN'T REALLY OVER. IT WAS BRUTAL IN THAT RING, AND IT LEFT BOTH ALI AND JOE EXHAUSTED AND INJURED.

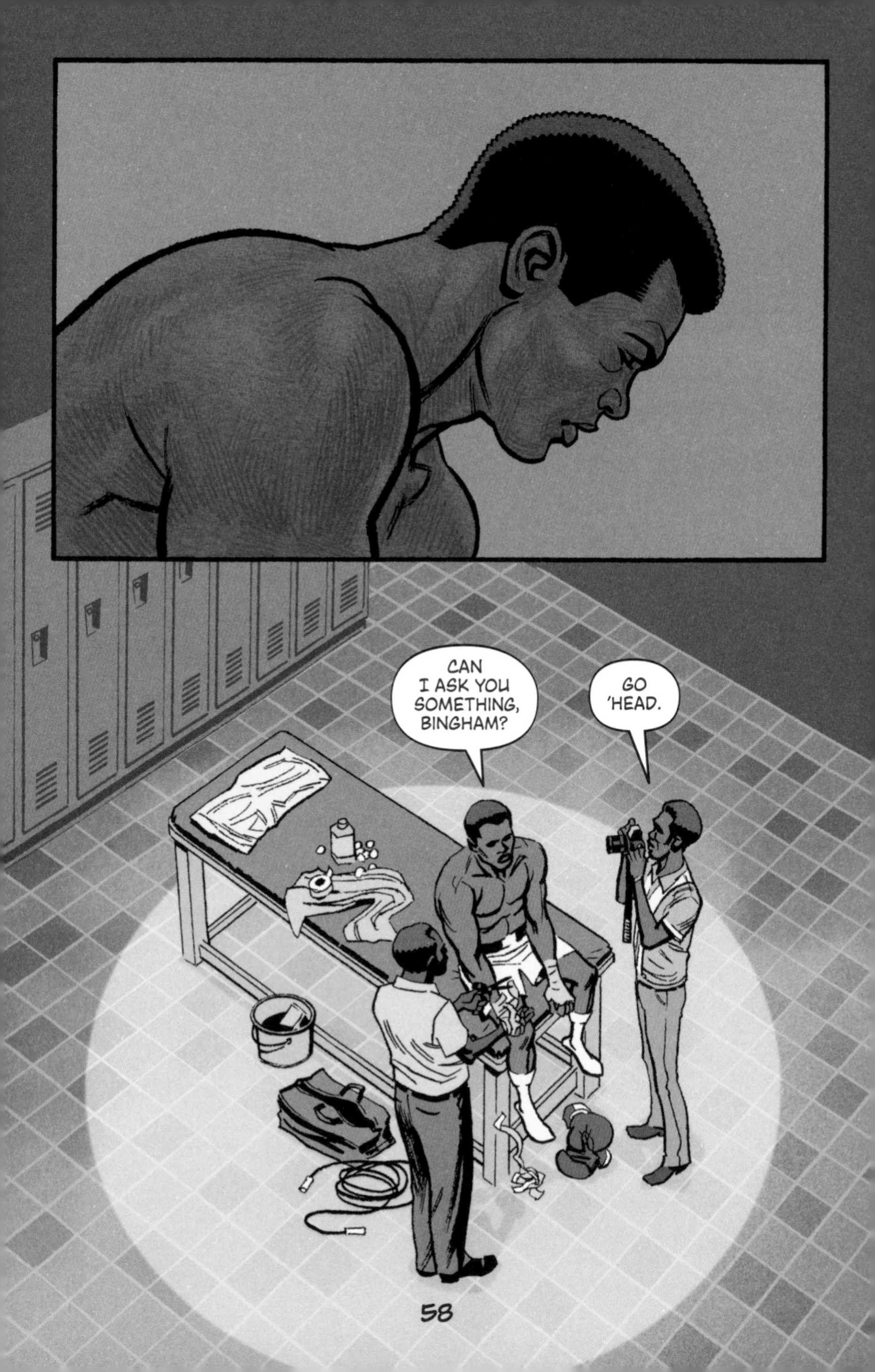
CAN I ASK YOU SOMETHING, BINGHAM?
GO 'HEAD.

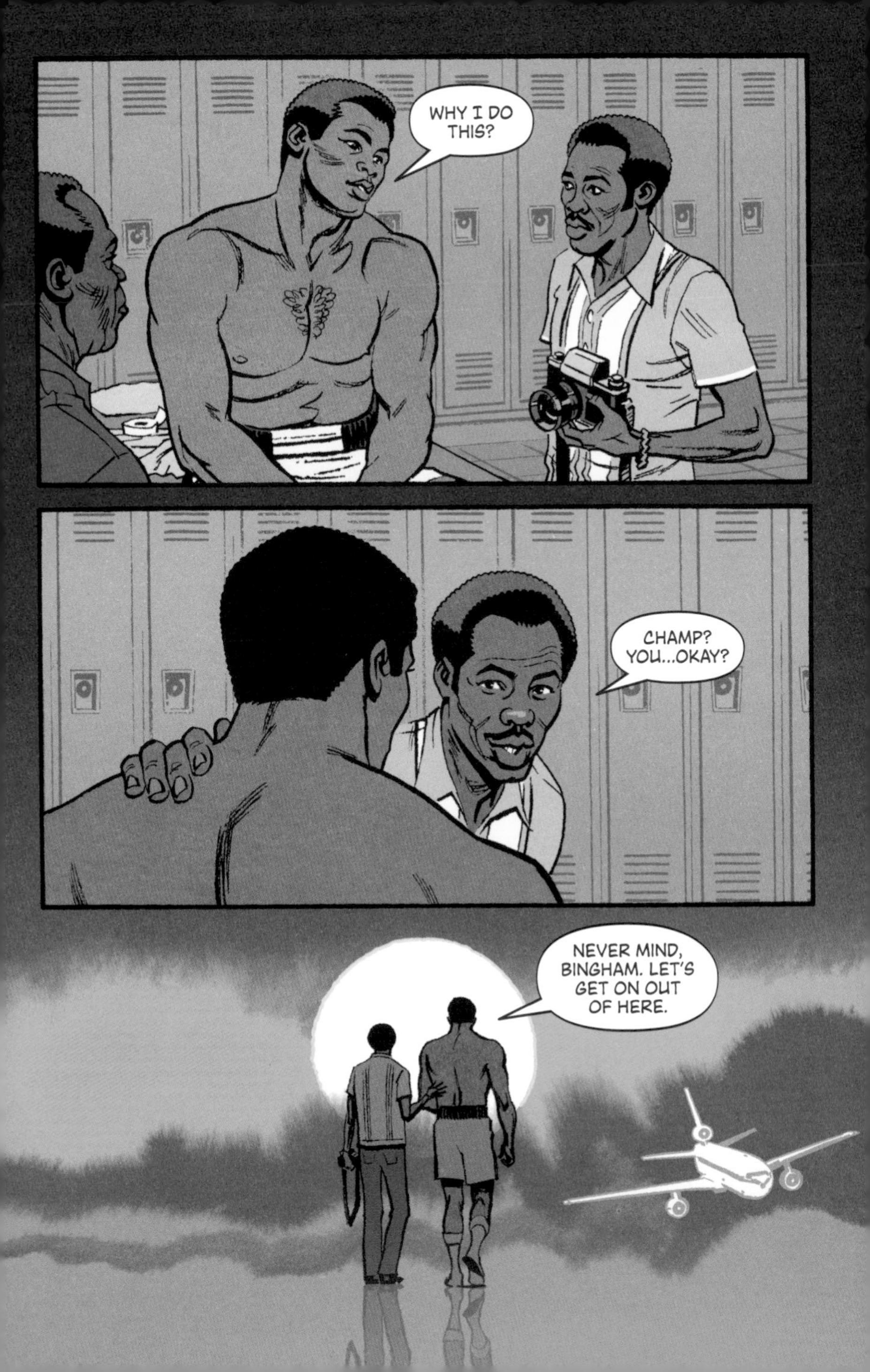
WHY I DO THIS?
CHAMP? YOU...OKAY?
NEVER MIND, BINGHAM. LET'S GET ON OUT OF HERE.

Conclusion

After the Thrilla in Manila, Ali's fighting career continued in the ring, as well as on the screen, when he portrayed himself in the 1977 movie *The Greatest*, and on the page in the 1978 comic book *Superman vs. Muhammad Ali*. Three years later, in 1981, Ali finally put his gloves away, retiring from the sport at the age of thirty-nine. Throughout it all, Howard Bingham and Muhammad Ali remained close friends, and Bingham was a constant presence by Ali's side for the rest of their lives.

After his retirement, Ali continued his work as an activist, goodwill ambassador, and civil rights advocate, even when he was diagnosed with the neurological disorder Parkinson's disease in the 1980s. In 1996, he lit the opening torch at the Olympic Games held in Atlanta. In 2001, his life was once again the subject of a film, titled *Ali*, and this time he was played by actor Will Smith.

The Thrilla in Manila lives on as one of the most physical, brutal, and greatest fighting matches in the history of professional boxing. "It was like death. Closest thing to dyin' that I know of," Ali later said of the event. In fact, the rift between Ali and Frazier never completely healed after the fight, though when Joe Frazier died in 2011, Ali attended his funeral. And even though Ali would go on to defend his title six more times, it would never be the same as that one electrifying October day in the Philippines.

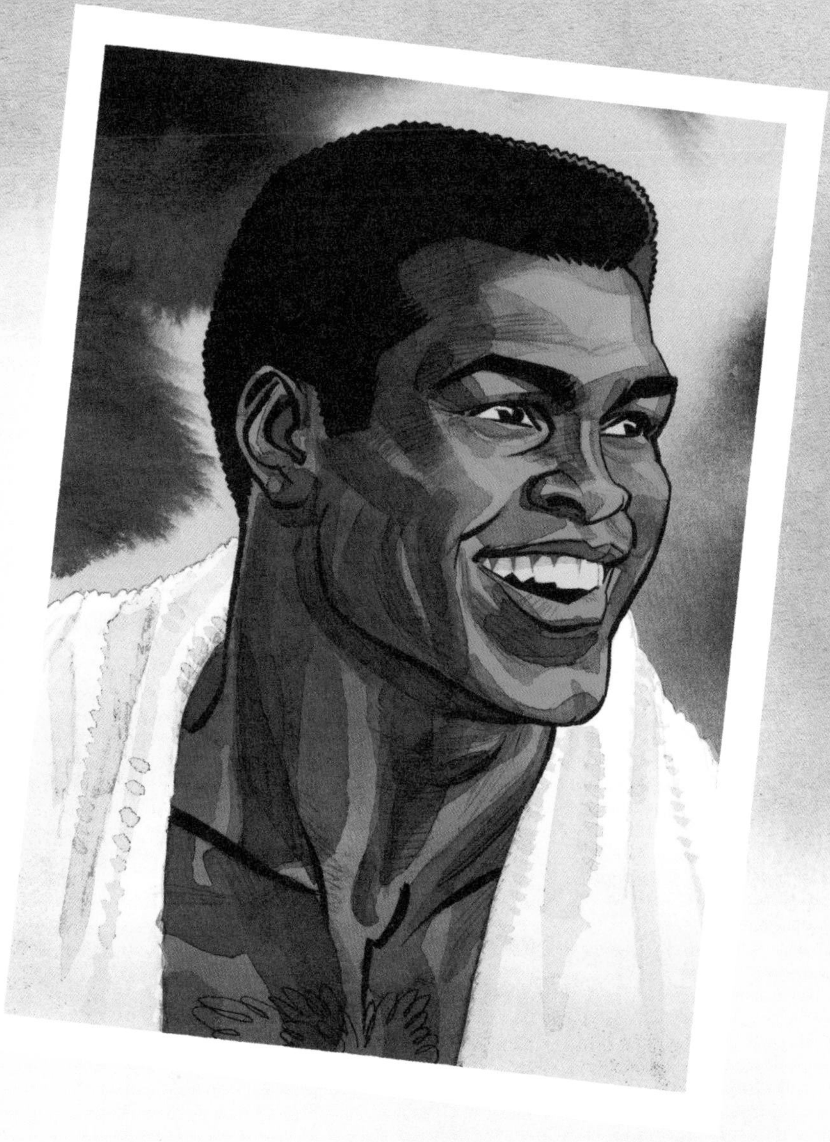

Timeline of Muhammad Ali's Life

1942 — Born Cassius Clay Jr. in Louisville, Kentucky

1954 — Begins to box

1959 — Wins Golden Gloves, his first major championship

1960 — Wins Olympic gold medal

1964 — Joins the Nation of Islam and changes his name to Muhammad Ali

1967 — Arrested for refusing to join army and charged with draft evasion

1970 — Returns to boxing

1971 — The US Supreme Court overturns Ali's conviction

— Defeated by Joe Frazier in their first fight at Madison Square Garden

1974 — Defeats Joe Frazier in their second fight at Madison Square Garden

— Defeats George Foreman in the Rumble in the Jungle

1975 — Defeats Joe Frazier in the Thrilla in Manila

1981 — Retires from boxing

1984 — Diagnosed with Parkinson's disease

2005 — Awarded the Presidential Medal of Freedom

— The Muhammad Ali Center opens in Louisville

2016 — Dies in Phoenix, Arizona

Bibliography

*Books for young readers

Bingham, Howard. *Muhammad Ali: A Thirty-Year Journey*. New York: Simon & Schuster, 1993.

*Buckley Jr., James. *Who Was Muhammad Ali?* New York: Penguin Workshop, 2014.

Early, Gerald, ed. *The Muhammad Ali Reader*. Hopewell, NJ: Ecco Press, 1998.

Eig, Jonathan. *Ali: A Life*. Boston: Houghton Mifflin Harcourt, 2017.

Frazier, Joe, with Phil Berger. *Smokin' Joe: The Autobiography*. New York: Macmillan, 1996.

Gast, Leon, dir. *When We Were Kings*. 1996. New York: Criterion, 2019. Blu-ray.

Hauser, Thomas. *Muhammad Ali: His Life and Times*. New York: Simon & Schuster, 1991.

Howard, Gregory Allen, Michael Mann, Stephen J. Rivele, and Diana Landau. *Ali: The Movie and the Man*. New York: Newmarket Press, 2001.

Kram, Mark. *Ghosts of Manila*. New York: HarperCollins, 2001.

Kram, Mark. *Smokin' Joe: The Life of Joe Frazier*. New York: HarperCollins, 2019.

Reed, Ishmael. *The Complete Muhammad Ali*. Montreal: Baraka Books, 2015.

Remnick, David. *King of the World*. New York: Vintage, 1999.

West, David, ed. *The Mammoth Book of Muhammad Ali*. Philadelphia: Running Press, 2012.

ABOUT THE CREATORS

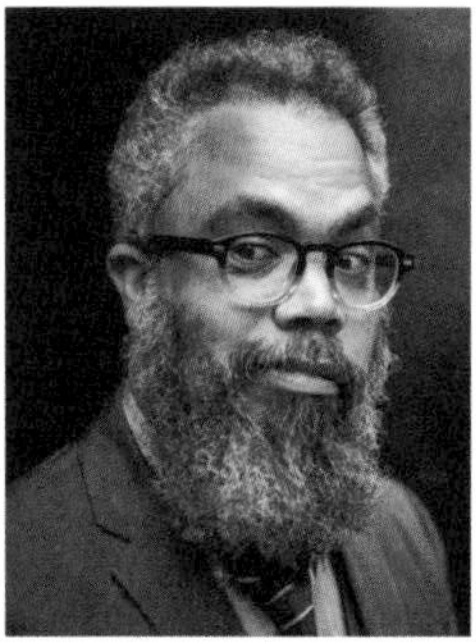

STEVE BURNS

Gabe Soria is best known in the kidlit community for reinventing the choice-driven book genre with his four-book series, Midnight Arcade. He has also written several comic books for DC Comics, including *Batman '66*, and has collaborated with the Black Keys' Dan Auerbach on the *Murder Ballads* comic book.

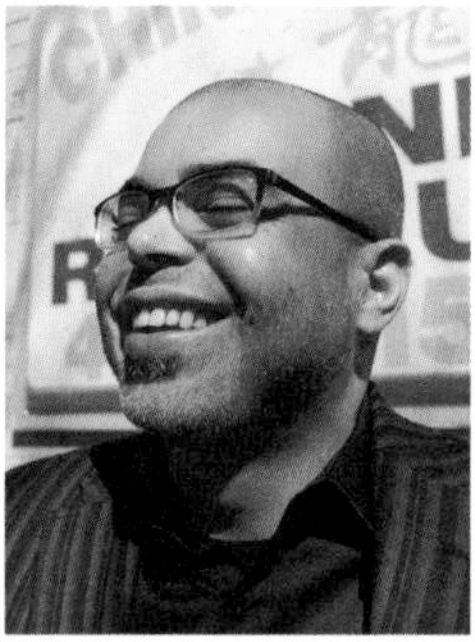

SHAWN CRYSTAL

Chris Brunner is a cartoonist based in Atlanta, Georgia. His clients have included Nike, Lucasfilm, Disney, Nickelodeon, the NBA, DC Comics, Marvel, and Image Comics. In 2016, he received his MFA from SCAD-Atlanta and is currently a professor in their Sequential Art department. His work contributed to the Eisner-winning *Southern Bastards* and *Bitter Root*, each awarded Best Ongoing Series in 2016 and 2020.

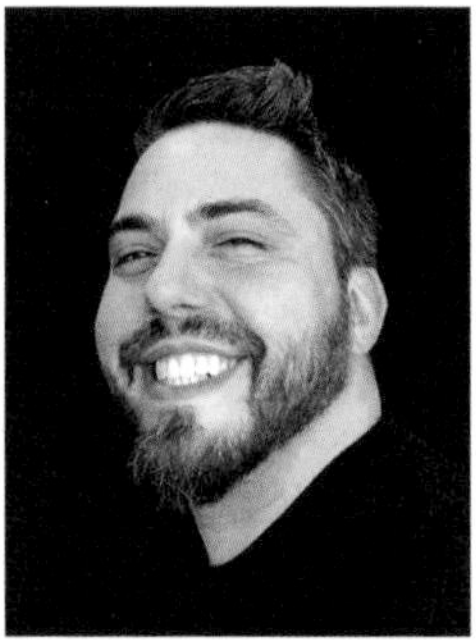

Rico Renzi is an artist and designer from Washington, DC. His work has appeared in *WIRED* and *Fast Company*, and various publications from DC Comics, Marvel, Image Comics, Dark Horse Comics, Scholastic, BOOM! Studios, Oni Press, and IDW. In 2018, his work was featured in *Spider-Man: Into the Spider-Verse*, which won the Oscar for Best Animated Feature Film at the 2019 Academy Awards.